D1130868

THE TREATY OF PORTSMOUTH

The TREATY *of* PORTSMOUTH

An Adventure in American Diplomacy

by

EUGENE P. TRANI

UNIVERSITY OF KENTUCKY PRESS

Printed in the U.S.A. Library of Congress Catalog Card No. 69-19767

TO THE MEMORY OF

Lt. Frederick E. Trani, Jr., USN

1940-1968

Preface

Theodore Roosevelt has always had a great deal of fascination as an individual but has rarely received attention as a diplomat. Certainly one of the most spectacular episodes of his diplomacy was the Treaty of Portsmouth. My interest in the event itself, as well as in Roosevelt's general thoughts and actions toward the governments of Russia and Japan, led to this study.

I would like to thank Robert Bremner, G. Wallace Chessman, Donald Davis, Raymond A. Esthus, Walter Nugent, Coen Pierson, and Fritz T. Epstein for their assistance. Chong Kun Yoon of Washington, D.C., helped me with the translation of the Japanese documents. Peter Coleman of the University of Illinois, Chicago Circle, gave the manuscript a close reading. I want to thank Thomas Wilson and the Piscataqua History Club for the assistance given me during my visits to Portsmouth and for permission to use photographs from the History Club's fine pictorial collection. But most of all to Robert Ferrell of Indiana University I am deeply indebted. This careful scholar has done much for me and this study. He has taught, aided, and advised me in so many ways. Only those who have had the experience of studying under Professor Ferrell realize the proportions of my debt. Finally, it is difficult, indeed impossible, to convey adequately my gratitude to my wife Lois for her help and understanding in this project, and in everyday life.

Contents

Illustrations

Chapter One

ROOSEVELT THE DIPLOMAT

A smack of Lord Cromer, Jeff Davis a touch of him;
A little of Lincoln, but not very much of him;
Kitchener, Bismarck, and Germany's Will,
Jupiter, Chamberlain, Buffalo Bill.[1]

THEODORE ROOSEVELT surely was one of the ornaments of the American political system, both for what he did as president and the way he lived as an individual. Much about him is familiar: "the teeth, the famous intensity, the nervous grimace, impelling leadership, physical courage, moral fervor—sometimes frenzy. . . . There are the busted trusts, the outdoor life, the nature fakirs, simplified spelling, rivers discovered, lions felled."[2] But this man has been more remembered than studied, especially his views on foreign affairs where to carry a big stick while speaking softly remains too easy an appraisal.

Of all functions of the presidency, none fascinated Roosevelt more than did foreign affairs. World responsibilities enraptured him; he went out of his way to accept tasks. Impatiently he viewed the slow reaction of his fellow Americans to the world struggle for power in the hectic phase prior to the First World War. He always acted, of course, to promote the American national interest as he saw it. He seldom consulted Congress on foreign policy—only when he felt a legal obligation—and was willing to stretch executive power to its limits and sometimes beyond. More than any other American of his time he assisted in the emergence of the United States as a world power. As president he won much recognition for his country, and diplomatic achievements crowded his presidential years as the United States dominated Latin America, pushed into European politics, protected interests in the Far East, modernized its army, increased its battle fleet, and pursued a generally enlightened policy toward new colonial dependencies. In the year 1905 alone—a banner year—Roosevelt, whom Henry Adams once unkindly described as pure act, helped arrange the Algeciras Conference which met in 1906, took charge of Santo Domingo, set up an engineering organization for the Panama Canal, and, most important, brought about, directed, and concluded the Peace of Portsmouth.

A new feeling of manifest destiny, opening an exciting epoch of American foreign affairs, had swept over the country at the end of the nineteenth century, and Theodore Roosevelt found himself caught up in it. This expansive feeling had philosophical roots quite in contrast to the old manifest destiny of the 1840s and 1850s: it traced to Charles Darwin's *On the Origin of Species* and gloried in such phrases as natural selection, survival of the fittest, struggle for existence. Advocates of the new manifest destiny believed that the United States, as a result of its successful establishment as a world power, was a fit nation, a chosen nation, qualified to instruct backward nations. Advocates of this idea believed that America should have possessions in the Caribbean, Pacific, and Orient. Theirs was a carbon copy of the European imperialism then prevalent in Asia and Africa. During the administrations of Presidents Grover Cleveland, Benjamin Harrison, and William McKinley, the United States government involved itself in diplomatic crises throughout the world. It opposed Great Britain and especially Germany in Samoa so as to obtain the harbor

[1] Mark Sullivan, *Our Times,* 6 vols. (New York, 1927-1935), II, 391.
[2] John M. Blum, *The Republican Roosevelt* (Cambridge, Mass., 1961), 1.

of Pago Pago. From Chile came $75,000 in indemnity and an apology for the killing in Valparaiso of two crewmen and the injuring of sixteen others of the cruiser *Baltimore*. Hawaii passed under American dominion, annexed in 1898. Cleveland in 1895-1896 forced Lord Salisbury's government to arbitrate the boundary between British Guiana and Venezuela. The century closed with the Spanish-American War.

As a young man Theodore Roosevelt accepted all this heady doctrine. His views on foreign policy were complicated but definite. He had grown up in a family that had known Europe firsthand. He traveled abroad as a youth, and not only made leisurely journeys through Europe and the Near East but lived for months in Rome, Paris, and Dresden. Except for the Adams family, Thomas Jefferson, and James Monroe, he was more traveled than any president who preceded him in office. More important, perhaps, he had developed not merely an acquaintance with Europeans but a genuine liking for them.

As the nineteenth century drew to a close and the American government appeared formidably on the world scene, Roosevelt urged expansion. Above all, he wanted to uphold the honor and interests of the United States. His writings displayed intense nationalism.[3] "I am not hostile to any European power in the abstract," he once said. "I am simply an American first and last, and therefore hostile to any power which wrongs us."[4]

He also basked in a belief in Anglo-Saxon superiority. He had studied at the Columbia University Law School under Professor John W. Burgess, who advocated the special ability of Anglo-Saxons to rule backward peoples. In reviewing Charles H. Pearson's *National Life and*

[3] Theodore Roosevelt, *The Naval War of 1812* (New York, 1924).

[4] Theodore Roosevelt to Francis C. Moore, Feb. 9, 1898, Theodore Roosevelt MSS in the Library of Congress; hereafter cited as TR MSS.

Character: A Forecast, Roosevelt in 1894 noted that peace had to be brought about in the world's waste spaces. Peace could not be had until the civilized nations expanded in some shape over the barbarous nations. He justified the exclusion of Chinese immigrants by noting that the American democracy with much clearness of vision had seen their presence as ruinous to the white race.[5] He admired the Japanese because they had kept only the strongest of their traditions and scrapped the rest. To be sure, other backward races could attain superior qualities and then command respect.[6]

While he believed in only a just war, any war in which Americans fought would be just, and he described the Spanish-American War as the most righteous war of the century.[7] America's leaders, as a result, had to have fighting qualities. "All the great masterful races have been fighting races," he once said, "and the minute that a race loses the hard fighting virtues, then . . . no matter how skilled in commerce and finance, in science and art, it has lost its proud right to stand as the equal of the best."[8]

More than any other person Captain Alfred Thayer Mahan, the author of *The Influence of Sea Power upon History* and the well-known promoter of the American navy, influenced Roosevelt's thinking on foreign affairs. Mahan's ideas were a starting point for almost every conversation Roosevelt held on foreign policy.

After the Spanish-American War, Roosevelt's view of the world became more complex, for he saw that the great powers could clash with each other as well as with colonial peoples, realized that power struggles in such places as East Asia influenced the balance of power in

[5] *Sewanee Review,* II (1894), 366.

[6] *Ibid.,* 367.

[7] "Fellow-Feeling as a Political Factor," *Century Magazine,* LIX (1900), 466.

[8] Address Before the Naval War College, June 2, 1897, TR MSS.

Europe, learned that the same nation threatening American interests in one area might share interests in another. He came to believe that America as a world power should try to increase its strength while preventing any nation from threatening the United States or its friends, and he warned that "we cannot sit huddled within our borders and avow ourselves merely an assemblage of well-to-do hucksters who care nothing for what happens beyond."[9] No longer did he gauge events solely in terms of American interests. As president he divided the world into a few great civilized powers, the purveyors of enlightenment and culture and protectors of law and order. These great nations, he observed with somewhat elementary acumen, engaged in a constant conflict for supremacy. As for the smaller civilized powers of Europe and the remaining nations, they occupied lower points in the scale of desirable national qualities.

There was an increasing shrewdness in the presidential remarks which is sometimes easy to forget when one notices the moral exhortations, the evangelical commentary that made Roosevelt seem an anachronism after he left the presidency. Bereft of rhetoric, his thoughts do not now, in the mid-twentieth century, seem so outdated. If presidential statements on foreign policy contained moral and ethical appeals, he understood that in absence of any accepted international law and an agency to enforce it the determinant in the world was power, and he became convinced that as long as nations existed, the loftiest ideals were worthless unless force backed them. A weak America invited destruction. He feared peace demagogues who preached disarmament. The president felt that nations should be equitable in dealings but quick to defend interests. The United States had to ensure its

[9] "The Strenuous Life," Address Before the Hamilton Club, April 10, 1899, in *The Strenuous Life: Essays and Addresses* (New York, 1903), 9.

new empire, including supremacy in the Caribbean, power in the Pacific, and a trans-Isthmian canal for easy movement of the navy from ocean to ocean.

Roosevelt became keenly aware of the changing structure of power, and if he lacked the capacity to look into the fateful future he sensed the seriousness of world politics. He beheld a declining Britain and rising Germany and Japan. The shifts of power convinced him that the United States would have to hold the balance of power if England failed to hold it, no matter against what countries. It was with an approving nod that Roosevelt had observed the United States and Britain come to an understanding in the last years of the McKinley era, largely due to the work of John Hay, secretary of state. Roosevelt believed the two countries had to think and act as one. When as president he occasionally scolded the British it was not over any difficulties themselves but because there was contention.

The decline of Great Britain was most clearly apparent at that time in East Asia where Russians, Japanese, Germans, and French were hastily and, as it turned out, thoughtlessly carving spheres of territorial and commercial influence. Western interest in China had increased throughout the nineteenth century; in the beginning motives were those of christianizing and civilizing, but by the middle of the century the motive was trade. China was weak, the Manchu dynasty in decline, the Opium War and the Taiping rebellion and Nien Fei uprisings all showed weakness. Still, China remained a nation, despite the invaders. Roosevelt's view of China was affected by economics and religion but primarily resulted from the thoughts of an international strategist. He realized that the struggle over China by the major powers was only one part of the world struggle. He came to know a good deal about China, its internal and external problems, had close friends who had spent years in Asia, and on the basis of their experience came to the conclusion that China could not control its destiny. The Chinese lacked cohesiveness, and the China problem would be longstanding.

China's defeat by the Japanese in 1895 announced the new era in which China turned into a scene of wild scrambling for spheres of interest. The Russians received the right to build the Trans-Siberian railway through Manchuria and to construct naval facilities at Port Arthur. The Germans got Kiaochow, the French Kwangchow-wan, the British Wei-hai-wei. These concessions disturbed Roosevelt because they seemed to endanger American interests which had become important in the latter part of the nineteenth century and were increasing when he assumed the presidency.

In the area around China two nations in addition to the United States had become powerful—Russia and Japan. Initially Roosevelt had not been hostile toward the Russians, ties had been cordial, and he was aware as a student of history that Russia during the American Revolution had shown its friendship. The Russians had backed the North in the Civil War. They had sold Alaska. This procession of events led Roosevelt to write in 1898 that "Russia, and Russia alone, of European powers, has been uniformly friendly to us in the past."[10] In the 1890s he argued with his friend Sir Cecil Spring Rice, a British diplomat, who believed that the Russians imperiled British concerns in Persia, India, and China. Roosevelt passed off the admonition, saying that "even if in the dim future Russia should take India and become the preponderant power of Asia, England would merely be injured in one great dependency."[11] Shortly before becom-

[10] TR to Charles A. Moore, Feb. 14, 1898, TR MSS.
[11] TR to Cecil Spring Rice, Aug. 5, 1896, TR MSS.

ing president he changed his views. Russian Far Eastern encroachments about the time of the Boxer rebellion, according to him, were challenging Anglo-American interests. The powers had moved troops into China, and Russia with its long Chinese border virtually had occupied Manchuria. Russian expansion had become an obstacle. Because British power was in decline, America had to block the Russians. Roosevelt by 1903 was disturbed with the Russians for failing to withdraw from Manchuria. So was Secretary of State Hay who was writing that "dealing with a government with whom mendacity is a science is an extremely difficult and delicate matter." Both the president and Hay realized that public opinion would support no scheme of military action with the British.[12] Washington tried to exert economic pressure and on the scheduled date of the final Russian evacuation of Manchuria, October 8, 1903, signed an agreement with the Chinese for the opening of new commerce in Manchuria. In the meantime another event colored Roosevelt's feelings for Russia. There was an outbreak of violence in Kishinev against the Jews in April 1903. Roosevelt publicly criticized Tsar Nicholas II and the Russian autocracy. Months later he wrote to Spring Rice of "a strong liking and respect" for the Russians "but unless they change in some marked way they contain the chance of menace to the higher life of the world. . . . Our people have become suspicious of Russia; and I personally share this view."[13]

[12] John Hay to TR, May 12, 1903, John Hay MSS in the Library of Congress. This whole issue—the differences in Japanese and American policy that made Tokyo ready to resort to arms while Washington was unwilling—is well detailed in Raymond A. Esthus, *Theodore Roosevelt and Japan* (Seattle, 1966), 7-20. Esthus carefully analyzes American policy from 1900 to 1905. He points out that American interest in the preservation of Chinese integrity was largely commercial, while the Japanese interest was primarily strategic. While Washington looked at Russia in Manchuria, Tokyo viewed with alarm the move of the Russians from Siberia to Manchuria to Korea.

[13] TR to Spring Rice, Feb. 2, 1904, TR MSS; see also TR to George Otto Trevelyan, March 9, 1905, TR MSS.

When the Russo-Japanese War began in 1904 he asked the navy for a plan "in case it became necessary for our Asiatic squadron to bottle up the Vladivostok Russian squadron. I do not anticipate the slightest trouble, but . . . I want to be prepared for emergencies."[14]

Toward the Japanese the president's feelings likewise shifted. Through his public life he was torn between admiration for Japanese efficiency and fighting qualities and fear of the country's strength in war. Upon Japan's protest at the possible annexation of Hawaii by the United States in 1897 the then assistant secretary of the navy had declared, "The United States is not in a position which requires her to ask Japan or any other foreign Power what territory it shall or shall not acquire."[15] After the Spanish-American War, Roosevelt worried about the Philippine Islands. In the years 1900-1905 his admiration overcame fear, and he became convinced that the Island Empire did not threaten American interests. Unprepared to use force to stop the Russian advance, he saw the Japanese as a barrier. When the Japanese protested Russian policy in Manchuria, Roosevelt was sympathetic. Japan was not only a protector of the open door but of the balance of power. He had approved of the alliance between Japan and Britain concluded in 1902; he realized that the American people would not accept participation in the alliance, which would have been a break from past policy, but the alliance did offer protection for his country.

Roosevelt's peculiarly personal handling of foreign policy during his presidency began in the years 1904-1905, the time of his mediation between the Russians and Japanese, and of his negotiation of the Peace of Portsmouth. Up until this time foreign policy had been under control of one of the few elder statesmen among Roose-

[14] TR to John E. Pillsbury, July 29, 1904, TR MSS.

[15] Speech to the Ohio Naval Reserves, New York *Tribune,* July 27, 1897, TR Scrapbooks, TR MSS.

velt's advisers in and out of the cabinet, John Hay. Hay had served in his youth as one of Abraham Lincoln's secretaries and aides, as a member of the legations in Paris, Vienna, and Madrid, as an editor for the New York *Tribune,* and as an assistant secretary of state under President Rutherford B. Hayes. All the while he was gaining a reputation as an author—with John G. Nicolay he had written a biography of Lincoln, and also had composed *Pike County Ballads* and the well-known poem "Jim Bludsoe." McKinley appointed Hay ambassador to London in 1897 and then made him secretary of state. In the latter position Hay was a tower of moderation for the president. Roosevelt respected Hay, and they developed a tender affection. Sundays on return from church the young president would drop in on Hay at the large graystone house on Jackson Place for an hour's discussion of affairs of state. Sometimes they were alone, other times with such friends as William Howard Taft or Elihu Root. Hay by 1904 was failing physically, and he died in the summer of 1905. For some years he was of a morbid caste of mind, if with reason, and had written of his premonitions in a pro forma letter of resignation to the new president after McKinley's death: "My official life is at an end—my natural life will not be long extended: and so, in the dawn of what I am sure will be a great and splendid future, I venture to give you the heartfelt benediction of the past."[16] Roosevelt refused the resignation, urging Hay to remain until 1904. In the autumn of that year Hay went to Europe for a vacation, and Roosevelt commenced acting as secretary of state. By the spring of 1905 the president was writing diplomatic notes which he sent over to the State Department, next door to the White House, for transmission to envoys abroad. One should note that the president never had large differences of

[16] Hay to TR, Sept. 15, 1901, TR MSS.

opinion over policy with Hay, and the major difference in conduct of the State Department was in technique.

Roosevelt's diplomacy was so personal that there were times when Mrs. Roosevelt was the president's adviser. For three important weeks in June 1905, during negotiations of the Peace of Portsmouth, the State Department did not know that the Japanese government had asked Roosevelt for a direct negotiation. Roosevelt had all the personal touch of the other figures of his day: Théophile Delcassé, Bernhard von Bülow, Sir Edward Grey among the foreign ministers, and the two leading monarchs Wilhelm II and Edward VII. Like them he was not the sole builder of the policy of his country from 1900, for some ideas and practices came from the McKinley administration, some from subordinates, many out of the complex situation of the world; yet his was the controlling hand.[17]

Roosevelt had a saving grace in his behavior, without which he might have seemed like a posturer on the world stage: he had an acute sense of the ridiculous, of the absurd. This is a point worth mentioning in some detail. He lived, after all, in the era of great strutters and posers, the Mary Gardens and Dame Nellie Melbas of international relations, and he might have been tempted to act as they did. Mary Garden, it was often said, had no voice, but could act. He could have fashioned himself after the military figures of his day such as General Arthur MacArthur or the general's European equivalents. Instead there was always a feeling on his part that he might be pompous, and it kept him in the mainstream, so to speak, of American life.

The president disliked diplomatic formalities. He especially disliked the title Excellency referring to the president; he saw no need of a title. He wrote the Depart-

[17] William H. Harbaugh, *Power and Responsibility: The Life and Times of Theodore Roosevelt* (New York, 1961), 183.

ment of State that "any title is silly when given the President. This title is rather unusually silly. But it is not only silly but inexcusable for the State Department . . . to permit foreign representatives to fall into the blunder of using this title."[18] Procedural details irked him. The State Department became his target and he singled out as the bull's-eye Assistant Secretary Alvey A. Adee, who had written formal messages of the presidents since Chester A. Arthur. "I am always sending a congratulation, or a felicitation, or a message of condolence or sympathy to somebody in a palace somewhere or other, and old Adee does that for me. . . . Why, there isn't a kitten born in a palace anywhere on earth," he noted, "that I don't have to write a letter of congratulation to the peripatetic Tomcat that might have been its sire, and old Adee does that for me!"[19] He told American diplomats abroad to use commonsense in dress and to wear whatever would please the sovereign of the country they served. He enjoyed breaking up diplomatic traditions, such as the custom that prevented entertaining people of equal rank. He took the delight of a truant boy in forcing dignitaries into horseback rides in Rock Creek Park or walks up and down the wooded hills—his head upward to catch sight of birds, looking like a grotesquely burly Peter Pan while his visitors huffed and puffed.[20]

Apart from this lack of decorum Roosevelt differed from Hay in handling foreign relations by his manner of obtaining diplomatic information, for he put little faith in the regular envoys abroad. He went to bureau chiefs, head clerks, or anyone he trusted. The American diplomatic service of this time indeed was amateurish,

18 TR to Acting Secretary of State Alvey A. Adee, Sept. 2, 1904, and TR to State Department, Dec. 2, 1908, TR MSS.

19 Oscar King Davis, *Released for Publication* (Boston, 1925), 143-44; and TR to Hay, Sept. 9, 1902, TR MSS.

20 Sullivan, *Our Times*, II, 395.

full of old timber as Oscar Straus was to write, a result of a provincial Congress and the spoils system.[21] To George von Lengerke Meyer whom in 1905 he was to send from Rome to the embassy in St. Petersburg, the president wrote, "The trouble with our Ambassadors in stations of real importance is that they totally fail to give us real help and real information, and seem to think that the life work of an Ambassador is a kind of a glorified pink tea party."[22] As for Meyer's predecessor in St. Petersburg, Robert S. McCormick, a Chicago businessman and father of the later colonel, Roosevelt considered him politically important but diplomatically useless, a not unfair judgment.[23] The American minister in Tokyo, Lloyd C. Griscom, was a diplomat of experience who had been minister to Persia, but for some good reason he was not an important cog in Roosevelt's machine. Roosevelt kept Griscom almost as uninformed as certain European governments treated their Washington ambassadors, perhaps in a calculated presidential effort to maintain a balance of ignorance.[24] It is saddening to go through the dispatches to and from Griscom in Tokyo at the peak

21 Oscar Straus, "A Night at the White House as a Guest of the President," Nov. 16, 1904, unpublished description, Oscar Straus MSS in the Library of Congress.

22 TR to George von L. Meyer, Dec. 26, 1904, George von L. Meyer MSS in the Massachusetts Historical Society. The Meyer MSS in the Massachusetts Historical Society contain Meyer's personal letter collection. Hereafter this collection will be cited as Meyer MSS. His diaries for 1904 and 1905 are in the Manuscript Division, Library of Congress, and will be cited as Meyer MSS LC.

23 Straus, "A Night at the White House."

24 Straus to TR, March 15, 1905, TR MSS. The Roosevelt-Griscom relationship is a strange one. Griscom seems to have been quite important in Hay's diplomacy, and served valuable duty while Hay ran the State Department, especially in the prewar period. But with the war and Hay's decline, Griscom was edged out when Roosevelt took control of American diplomacy. This is another indication of the personal nature of Roosevelt's diplomacy. He did not know Griscom and took Japanese-American relations out of the minister's hands. For an analysis of Griscom's prewar importance, see Esthus, *Theodore Roosevelt and Japan,* chap. 1.

of the crisis over the peace treaty between Russia and Japan in 1904-1905, a negotiation that should have seen Griscom at its center, and observe the minister reporting American war claims against Japan, requesting tourist permits for Japanese to visit the United States, and even once asking for "another typewriter of the Remington pattern."[25] Griscom was so far out of prime diplomatic equations that Secretary of War Taft's visit to Japan in 1905 to discuss Japanese intentions toward the Philippines and Hawaii took him by surprise: "The summer was not so quiet as I had anticipated. Suddenly I had word that our Secretary of War, William Howard Taft, was to stop."[26] On the other side of the world there was no close presidential representation at the Court of St. James's during the negotiation ending the Russo-Japanese War; Joseph H. Choate, a longtime friend of the president, gave way to Whitelaw Reid in early 1905, but the latter did not reach London until too late to be of any help. Roosevelt in 1904-1905 wanted little or no action from his envoys to the other major capitals on the Continent, old General Horace Porter of Civil War fame in Paris and Charlemagne Tower in Berlin. Tower did little or nothing. Porter spent his time in France on a macabre research into old leaden coffins in an abandoned Paris graveyard, looking for the body of John Paul Jones: eventually he found a set of old bones that measured up to Jones' qualifications and sent them home for burial at the Naval Academy.[27]

As for the envoys available in Washington, Roosevelt also had problems. The Russian ambassador, Count

[25] Lloyd Griscom to Hay, April 28, 1904, Microfilms of State Department Archives in the National Archives; hereafter cited as SDA NA.

[26] Lloyd Griscom, *Diplomatically Speaking* (Boston, 1940), 257.

[27] See the Horace Porter MSS in the Library of Congress. They contain a complete record of Porter's search for Jones's body, including a number of pictures.

Arturo P. Cassini (grandfather of the later society columnist and playboy Igor and the dress designer Oleg), was not only difficult, he was a liar. Cassini was the dean of the diplomatic corps. He had a considerable personal experience in Russia's Far Eastern policy and it was unfortunate he was unable to use it. As minister in Peking he had made arrangements for the Li-Lobanov Treaty of 1896 between Russia and China, and assisted in negotiations regarding Russian evacuation of Manchuria in 1902, the failure of which was one of the causes of the Russo-Japanese War. But the Russian government also mistrusted its Washington envoy and left Cassini uninformed. Roosevelt sometimes knew Russia's plans before the ambassador.

With the other belligerent of 1904-1905, Japan, the Washington envoy presented a different problem. The president much preferred the Japanese minister, Kogoro Takahira, to Cassini. Takahira never once gave Roosevelt cause to regret this preference. Relations between the two were nonetheless a little too correct, for Takahira held himself rigidly to the diplomatic code and never took the liberty of addressing a communication directly to the president.[28]

There was a problem of communicating with the British, for while Ambassador Sir Mortimer Durand, an old India hand, was a qualified diplomat, Roosevelt did not take to him. Durand rode well and played a good game of cricket, but had no vigor for the hikes and swims in which the president gloried. In a diary the despondent ambassador described his failure:

We drove out to the Rock Creek, a wooded valley with a stream running through it, and he then plunged down the

[28] Tyler Dennett, *Roosevelt and the Russo-Japanese War* (Garden City, N. Y., 1925), 34.

khud, and made me struggle through bushes and over rocks for two hours and a half, at an impossible speed, till I was so done that I could hardly stand. His great delight is rock climbing, which is my weak-point. I disgraced myself completely, and my arms and shoulders are still stiff with dragging myself up by roots and ledges. At one place I fairly stuck, and could not get over the top till he caught me by the collar and hauled at me. . . . He did almost all the talking, to my great relief, for I had no breath to spare.[29]

So much did Durand arouse the hostility of the president that in 1906 Roosevelt complained, "Why, under Heaven the English keep him here I do not know! If they do not care for an Ambassador, then abolish the Embassy; but it is useless to have a worthy creature of muttonsuet consistency like the good Sir Mortimer."[30]

In contrast the German and French representatives in Washington were not only friends of the president but people he trusted and used in diplomatic dealings. Both Jean Jules Jusserand and Baron Hermann Speck von Sternburg played tennis, swam the chilly Potomac in springtime, crawled through the mud of Rock Creek, and scaled cliffs. Speck von Sternburg's friendship went back to the late 1880s when Roosevelt was a civil service commissioner and Speck von Sternburg a diplomatic secretary. When Roosevelt became president, he sought to get Speck von Sternburg named German ambassador, and in early 1903 Speck von Sternburg replaced Theodor von Holleben. Not as effervescent as some of TR's other friends, Speck von Sternburg had special qualities. Of him Roosevelt wrote: "he was a capital shot, rider, and walker, a devoted and most efficient servant of Germany, who had fought with distinction in the Franco-German War

[29] Diary of Mortimer Durand, as cited in Percy Sykes, *The Right Honourable Sir Mortimer Durand* (London, 1926), 275-76.

[30] TR to Whitelaw Reid, April 28, 1906, TR MSS.

when barely more than a boy."[31] His wife was American and his mother English, further endearing him to Roosevelt. As for France's contribution to Washington, Jusserand was a good athlete, a mountain climber, who learned to walk straight into rivers and mudholes and avoid paths and bridges with a feeling of horror.[32] Jusserand also had an American-born wife. He was a jokester, making friendship with the president even more probable. Once as they were about to go swimming *en naturel* in the Potomac, Roosevelt shouted: "Eh, Mr. Ambassador, have you not forgotten your gloves?" Jusserand replied he would leave them on, "we might meet ladies."[33]

For much diplomatic advice the president turned from the diplomatic corps, with the exception of Jusserand and Speck von Sternburg, to a group of friends gathered over the years, some owing allegiance to other governments—the famous Tennis cabinet, the band of men that helped shape American policy from 1901 until 1909, an outgrowth of an earlier circle of friends of the 1890s with which the youthful Roosevelt had exchanged truths and prejudices. The earlier circle had included Henry Cabot Lodge who had come to Congress in 1887 with a new Harvard Ph.D.; the Adams brothers Henry and Brooks; Rudyard Kipling; William W. Rockhill, an expert on Far Eastern Affairs who from 1896 to 1897 was assistant secretary of state; and Captain Mahan, for a while a lecturer at the Naval War College in Newport, Rhode Island. Over the years the circle increased. These ad-

31 Theodore Roosevelt, *An Autobiography* (New York, 1920), 31. There seems to be some controversy as to the spelling of the German ambassador's name. Many of the American sources, including Roosevelt's *An Autobiography*, and Elting E. Morison, *The Letters of Theodore Roosevelt*, 8 vols. (Cambridge, Mass., 1951-1954), spell the name Sternberg. But German sources spell the name Sternburg. See, for example, *Meyers Grosses Konversations-Lexikon*, 6th rev. ed. (Leipzig and Vienna, 1907), XVIII, 700. Roosevelt spelled the name Sternburg in the TR MSS.

32 Jean Jules Jusserand, *What Me Befell* (Boston, 1933), 330.

33 *Ibid.*, 335-36.

visers were likely to pop up like tennis balls anywhere from Washington to Vladivostok. When Roosevelt took charge of foreign affairs he turned to these friends. "While in the White House," he recalled, "I always tried to get a couple of hours' exercise in the afternoons—sometimes tennis, more often riding, or else a rough cross-country walk. . . . My companions at tennis or on these rides and walks we gradually grew to style the Tennis Cabinet."[34]

The first notable member, albeit in absentia, was George Meyer, already mentioned, appointed to St. Petersburg in December 1904. To solve the most difficult problem for the Peace of Portsmouth, communicating with the Russians, the president shifted McCormick from St. Petersburg to Paris, replacing Porter, and moved Meyer from Rome. McKinley in 1900 had named Meyer as ambassador to Rome. Later to serve Roosevelt as postmaster general, he was an old friend; the two men had attended Harvard together. He had wealth, charm, a will to work, an alert mind, and (unusual for an American ambassador) fluency in French and Italian. Roosevelt in his *Autobiography* said that, with the exception of Henry White, Meyer was the most useful diplomat in service, and that he rendered invaluable aid by seeing the tsar when Roosevelt could not act through the Russian representatives.[35] In a frank letter, not at all flattering to other ambassadors, the president told Meyer that St. Petersburg was the only embassy where he wanted work done at that time and Meyer was the man to do it.[36] Meyer was not happy and wrote in his diary that "the President had intended to send me to Paris. . . . I am sorry on account of my family."[37] Because of duties in

34 Roosevelt, *An Autobiography*, 45.
35 *Ibid.*, 543.
36 TR to Meyer, Dec. 26, 1904, Meyer MSS.
37 Diary of George Meyer, Jan. 7, 1905, Meyer MSS LC; see also Meyer to TR, Jan. 20, 1905, TR MSS.

Rome and a brief visit to Berlin at the president's request, he did not reach the Russian capital until April 1905, when the Russo-Japanese War almost had ended.

The Japanese government saw the importance of Roosevelt's friendship and during the war sent a special envoy to direct Japan's public relations in this country and cultivate Roosevelt's liking of things Japanese. Baron Kentaro Kaneko had been a schoolmate at Harvard, and became Japan's member of the Tennis cabinet.[38] He was a distinguished statesman, the son of an old Samurai family, who had been a professor at what later became Tokyo Imperial University. At one time he was private secretary to Marquis Hirobumi Ito and had served as president of the Privy Council, chief secretary of the House of Peers, and a delegate to the 1892 International Law Conference in Switzerland. Kaneko arrived in 1904 and set up an office in New York to maintain American good will, to explain the yellow peril, and, more important because the Japanese believed the United States the only acceptable candidate for a mediatory role, to keep Roosevelt on Japan's side.[39] This ambassador to the American people, as Hay referred to him, renewed old acquaintances and became an intimate of the president.[40] He explained Japan's goal in the war and Japanese history. Roosevelt was favorably impressed with this representative of a faraway land. At Kaneko's suggestion he read about Bushido

[38] New York *Times,* May 17, 1942. This is a short story on Baron Kentaro Kaneko on the occasion of his death.

[39] Jutaro Komura to Tadasu Hayashi, March 8, 1904 (#130), "Nichi-Ro Sen'eki kankei kakkoku yoron keihatsu no tame Suematsu, Kaneko ryō-Danshaku Ōbei e haken ikken" [Documents Relating to the Despatch of Barons Suematsu and Kaneko to Europe and the U.S. for the Purpose of Enlightening Public Opinion in Various Countries Regarding the Russo-Japanese War], Kaneko Reel MT804, Microfilms of the Japanese Foreign Ministry Archives in the Library of Congress. This letter explains in detail what purpose these unofficial representatives of the Japanese government were to serve; see also Griscom to Hay, Feb. 23, 1904, Hay MSS.

[40] Diary of John Hay, Jan. 4, 1905, Hay MSS.

and other topics.[41] So valuable was Kaneko that on his departure the president wrote no simple farewell note drafted by his master of routine Adee:

Will you permit me at this time to say to you how much I have enjoyed our intercourse during the last year and a half, and how deeply I appreciate the services you have rendered throughout that period in keeping our two countries in close touch? You have rendered me an invaluable assistance by the way in which you have enabled me to know at first hand so much that it was important for me to know, and also by the way in which you have enabled me to convey to your own Government certain things which I thought it desirable to have known and which I hardly cared to forward through official channels.[42]

Another member of the Tennis cabinet proved important for the Peace of Portsmouth, when, because of dissatisfaction with Durand and the unsettled situation of the embassy in London, Roosevelt negotiated with the British government through Spring Rice, then first secretary of the British embassy in St. Petersburg. Roosevelt had first met Spring Rice in late 1886, and a few weeks afterward this charter member of the Tennis cabinet had served as best man for Roosevelt's second marriage. During the Harrison administration, Spring Rice was secretary of the embassy in Washington. The two young men had

41 "Kaneko Dan to Bei Daitōryō to no kaiken shimatsu" [The Interviews between Baron Kaneko and the President of the United States], Kaneko Reel MT804, Microfilms of the Japanese Foreign Ministry Archives. This report to the Japanese Foreign Ministry describes the talks of the following dates: 1904: March 26, 28, June 6, Dec. 19; 1905: Jan. 7, 8, Feb. 26, March 20, May 18, June 7, Aug. 5, 7, 14, 18, 21, 25, and Sept. 10, as well as the Roosevelt meeting of July 28, 1905, with Komura and Takahira. The frequency of the visits plus the topics discussed clearly show Roosevelt's pro-Japanese feelings. See also Kentaro Kaneko, *Nichiro seneki hiroku* [Secret Records of the Russo-Japanese War] (Tokyo, 1929), a compilation of three lectures Kaneko gave in which he described his relationship with Roosevelt.

42 TR to Kaneko, Sept. 11, 1905, TR MSS.

played tennis daily and settled the affairs of the world as young bureaucrats are prone to do. Roosevelt as president tried to have Spring Rice made ambassador to Washington, after the death of Sir Michael Herbert (also a member of the Tennis cabinet), but Lord Henry Lansdowne, the foreign secretary, knew Durand and his desire to go to America, liked him, and would hear nothing of it. For British correspondence the president therefore used the absurd route of Washington to St. Petersburg to London and back.

Two other Tennis cabinet members contributed to Roosevelt's decisions on foreign policy, especially during the Russo-Japanese War. Roosevelt inherited Elihu Root from McKinley as secretary of war. He rated Root as one of the wisest, most farseeing, ablest Americans of his day. He recognized the success achieved by Root in the War Department. Root initiated basic reforms in the army, bringing it to a better stage of preparation. He established the Army War College, reorganized the national guard, and introduced the general staff system. In addition to making the department efficient, Root had organized the American empire in the Caribbean and the western Pacific which resulted from the Spanish-American War. He brought order to the troubled Philippines, helped set up governments in Cuba and Puerto Rico, and did all in his power to bring fair and equal treatment to these new subjects of the United States. Root also had a sense of humor, and got along well with Roosevelt. The relationship between the two men was cordial because Root never competed with the president; he made no attempt to overshadow his chief. The president on his side regarded Root as a counterweight to his own hasty manner. Root in a sense began to replace Hay as the senior statesman in the cabinet, though only slightly older than the president. After almost five years in the cabinet, 1899-1904, Root in February 1904 returned to his law practice.

Roosevelt was saddened and wrote, "I shall never have, and can never have, a more loyal friend, a more faithful and wiser adviser, nor will the government ever be served by any man with greater zeal, efficiency and success."[43] Root was to hold no official position during much of the negotiation crisis, becoming secretary of state only upon Hay's death, but there was frequent communication between Washington and New York.

Perhaps the most important of all Roosevelt's advisers, Taft, had met the president during the Harrison administration when Taft was solicitor general. The two men lived near one another, visited back and forth, and walked to their offices together, passing the Executive Mansion as it then was called. Taft became a federal judge and dean of the law school of the University of Cincinnati, and then governor-general of the Philippines. Roosevelt was anxious to get Taft back to Washington, three times offering him positions on the Supreme Court. Taft finally agreed to replace Root in the cabinet. Upon his return in 1904 and with the departure of Root, he became Roosevelt's troubleshooter. Whenever a situation needed the solvent of good will or the oil of benevolence, or whenever wounded pride required the disinfectant of a laugh, Taft was the answer. No one felt comfortable disagreeing with him. He made Roosevelt feel secure. Nor was the president disturbed on hearing from the easy chair an audible sigh of recovery from the day's more strenuous labors. Roosevelt would beam the more, for he knew that when Taft relaxed everything must be all right.[44]

43 TR to Mrs. Elihu Root, Feb. 1, 1904, as cited in Charles Toth, "Elihu Root," in *An Uncertain Tradition: American Secretaries of State in the Twentieth Century,* ed. Norman Graebner (New York, 1961), 40; see also Sullivan, *Our Times,* III, 14.

44 Sullivan, *Our Times,* III, 4-20.

Chapter Two

1904: YEAR OF FRUSTRATION

Good old year of nineteen-four!
Every one had goods in store—
Wheat galore, a dollar up,
Lots to eat and lots to sup.
None abroad is mad at us;
Naught at home to cause a fuss—
May the year ahead give more
Of the brand of nineteen-four![1]

THE YEAR 1904 offered no settlement to the Far Eastern war. It was a strange time for diplomatic frustration, since in so many other ways the year marked a happy time for citizens of the United States and many people the world over. Perhaps it is true that individuals do not understand how well off they are until some catastrophe befalls them. Then they look back to the "good old days." People in the United States or elsewhere in 1904 probably looked back to the 1890s. But even in long retrospect it appears as if the year 1904, ten years before the outbreak of World War I, marked one of those brief moments when international affairs had not become too serious and people could carry out many of their aims and ambitions, at least if they had patience and the money.

In some respects that year 1904 was a simple time of sailor suits and long white dresses, of black Sunday clothes and double-lined finery. Little did Americans know that the Russo-Japanese War, which had opened early in the year with a surprise Japanese attack on the

Russian fleet at Port Arthur, would set in motion a train of calamities that in Asia and especially in Europe would upturn the world's international order for the next sixty years or more. Americans had learned of the Far East at the time of Commodore George Dewey's victory at Manila Bay, and read in 1904 that their president was seeking to arrange peace in Asia; that latter datum struck them as interesting, perhaps fascinating. It seemed a long way from the daily work in office or factory or the fields, and from planning for the long peaceful future.

The labyrinthine maneuverings of the European powers had encouraged war between Russia and Japan. Conflict in the Far East was part of the power struggle in Europe. The Russo-Japanese War had loomed over the international landscape for several years before it came into view, and its possibility saw the European powers with mixed sympathies and purposes. Ever since Germany's unification through the victory in the Franco-Prussian War of 1870-1871, the balance of power had been awry. Alliance systems, defensive and offensive, preoccupied the chancelleries of Europe. The Germans under Bismarck had remade Europe but not settled the politics of Europe. The French looked for revenge of their defeat. Bismarck had been able to isolate the French by alliances, first the Three Emperors' League and then the Triple Alliance. During this precarious balance the European nations had moved headlong into a course of imperialism, seeking raw materials, markets, prestige, and armed with bigger and more technologically advanced armies and navies. Then the new kaiser, Wilhelm II, dismissed the old diplomat Bismarck and the alliances underwent more changes.

By the turn of the century the European alignments were rigid, the tension in the Far East had increased perceptibly, and all aspiring nations were interested in

[1] Mark Sullivan, *Our Times*, 6 vols. (New York, 1927-1935), II, 631.

the increasing troubles between Russia and Japan. The French, Russia's allies since 1893-1894, were concerned about the conflict, for a Japanese victory over Russia would leave France's eastern border the main interest of the Germans and would imperil French investments in Russia derived from the loans of the 1890s—a fourth of all French foreign investment. The French government made a number of attempts to keep peace in Asia, the most important being in the autumn of 1903. Foreign Minister Delcassé acting on behalf of the Russians held serious discussions with Ichiro Motono, the Japanese minister in Paris.[2] But by early February 1904 the Japanese decided to break off the talks.[3] The French remained concerned, willing to do everything possible for peace, and were to make peace proposals throughout the war.

The British, Japan's allies since 1902, managed to offset any possible French assistance to the Russians. They had agreed to the alliance as protection for their Asian interests while they concentrated against Germany in Europe, and when the Russo-Japanese War began in 1904 they were thankful to see the Russian involvement, which took pressure off the borders of Persia and India. Just before the war Prime Minister Arthur Balfour had turned down Foreign Secretary Lansdowne's proposal to mediate. Balfour privately believed that the war would bring the Russians a limited victory but in the process thoroughly occupy them with the Far East.[4] By alliance with the

[2] Ichiro Motono to Komura, Jan. 16 (#260), Jan. 17 (#287), and Jan. 24, 1904 (#2329), and Komura to Motono, Jan. 14 (#2514), and Jan. 17, 1904 (#2518), Telegram Series, Reels for 1904, Japanese Foreign Ministry Archives.

[3] Komura to Shinichiro Kurino (St. Petersburg), Feb. 5 (#2289), and Feb. 5, 1904 (#2294), Telegram Series, Reels for 1904, Japanese Foreign Ministry Archives; see also McCormick to Hay, Feb. 7, 1904, and Griscom to Hay, Feb. 6, 1904, SDA NA.

[4] George Monger, *The End of Isolation: British Foreign Policy, 1900-1907* (London, 1963), 147-53.

Japanese the British, then, virtually prevented an intervention by the French. After the Far Eastern conflict opened, there was a slight chance that if a Russian defeat seemed near the French would risk a war with the British. The Anglo-French entente, signed in 1904 but talked about since April of the preceding year, eliminated this possibility; the entente seemed to settle the security needs of both countries—France against Germany, Britain against Russia. The chance of either nation's mediating in the Far Eastern war became too slight to consider.

The Germans at this time were the most unpredictable of the powers. Kaiser Wilhelm imagined a multitude of plots, all at expense of Germany, and disliked the Franco-Russian alliance; when he saw the possibility of an Anglo-French entente he tried to separate Russia from France by appealing to the monarchial principle. He wrote his cousin Tsar Nicholas in November 1903, "This shows you again, what I hinted at in our conversation, that the 'Crimean Combination' is forming and working against Russian interests in the East. 'The democratic countries governed by parliamentary majorities, against the Imperial Monarchies.' History allways [*sic*] will repeat itself."[5] He saw a Russo-Japanese War as an opportunity to involve the Russians (the ally of the French) against the Japanese (the ally of the British), believing that the new Anglo-French entente would force the breakup of the Franco-Russian alliance. He encouraged Nicholas to expand Russia's Far Eastern interests. In a letter of January 1904 he noted that "Korea must and will be Russian.

[5] Kaiser Wilhelm to Tsar Nicholas, Nov. 19, 1903, I. D. Levine, ed., *Letters from the Kaiser to the Czar* (New York, 1920); see also Hellmuth von Gerlach, ed., *Briefe und Telegramme Wilhelms II an Nikolaus II—1894-1914* (Berlin, 1920); and M. N. Pokrovsky, ed., *Perepiska Vilgelma vtorogo s Nikolaem vtorym* [Letters of Wilhelm II with Nicholas II] (Moscow, 1923). While the Levine edition is the best, since the kaiser wrote the letters in English, the other sources should be consulted, since they contain some of the tsar's answers.

When or how that is nobody's affair and concerns only you and your country."[6] The kaiser told his cousin that he should go to war, for otherwise he would endanger the monarchial principle and within twenty years see the yellow race in Moscow and Posen.[7] The German chancellor, Bülow, also urged Russia on, privately believing that the Russians' engagement in Eastern Asia would open up the Balkans to the Germans and Austrians.[8]

These sympathies of the European chancelleries drastically reduced the possibility of mediation by any of the European powers. Still, the Japanese worried about a French or German mediation, or even intervention. Tokyo could not forget that Paris, Berlin, and St. Petersburg had forbidden the Japanese conquests arising from the Treaty of Shimonoseki, which concluded the Sino-Japanese War in 1895. Another such intervention in 1900 had permitted the Russians to control Manchuria.

Besides the mediation of European governments there were other ways to bring peace, for example an international conference, although such a solution had limits. In the minds of all the statesmen was the recent Hague Peace Conference of 1899 which produced "paper achievements—masks concealing failure."[9] The Japanese were against such a meeting for the same reason they opposed

[6] Kaiser Wilhelm to Tsar Nicholas, Jan. 3, 1904, Levine, *Letters from the Kaiser to the Czar;* Pokrovsky, *Perepiska Vilgelma vtorogo s Nikolaem vtorym.*

[7] Secret Memorandum of Bernhard von Bülow, Feb. 14, 1904, Frederic Whyte, trans, and ed., *Letters of Prince von Bülow, 1903-1909* (London, 1930); see also Oakley Williams, trans. and ed., *Prince Bülow and the Kaiser* (London, 1932).

[8] Memorandum of Bülow, Jan. 16, 1904, which states that Germany should "avoid anything that might particularly awaken a suspicion in Russia that we are urging war," Bülow to Wilhelm II, Feb. 26, 1904, and Bülow to Below-Rutzau (Consul General in Serbia), March 29, 1904, Whyte, *Letters of Prince von Bülow;* see also Kurino to Komura, Jan. 1, 1904 (#12), Telegram Series, Reels for 1904, Japanese Foreign Ministry Archives.

[9] Calvin D. Davis, *The United States and the First Hague Peace Conference* (Ithaca, 1962), 213.

European meddling in the war. The Russians were not about to forget the conference of dishonest brokers that had revised the Treaty of San Stefano in Berlin in 1878, by which the tsarist regime lost virtually all influence over the Ottoman Empire and the Straits of Constantinople.

Another alternative was direct negotiation between the Japanese and Russians. As it turned out, this was no alternative because neither belligerent would make the first move, considering such a move an admission of defeat.

President Roosevelt watched the developing rivalries in Asia and kept his opinions to himself, though privately his sympathies lay with the Japanese. He believed that Tokyo was more likely to protect American interests. He saw the Far Eastern dispute as a conflict not for the independence of China and Korea but for control. The choice lay between dependence of China and Korea on the Russians, or on the Japanese. The Russians, as he told Spring Rice, would organize the provinces of North China, which they controlled economically, against American interests.[10]

And so he saw the Far Eastern giants move toward war. The Japanese had watched the Russians warily since the Triple Intervention of 1895. They were dismayed when they saw the Russians take the very concessions that the powers had forbidden the Japanese. Tokyo used the indemnity from China to modernize the army and navy. With the Boxer rebellion and Russian occupation of Manchuria the situation became critical. The Japanese refused to accept Russian control of this area so close to Japan. The blundering Russians made an effort to extend their influence into Korea at about the same time. The Japanese decision for war in 1904 was not made in haste. Tokyo had searched for diplomatic weapons to dislodge

[10] TR to Spring Rice, June 13, 1904, and Dec. 27, 1904, TR MSS.

the Russian menace and had gained the support of the British and even the Americans. The Japanese used this diplomatic front to make the Russians appear as aggressors, while the Japanese seemed interested only in protection of the Chinese empire. Soon the Japanese saw that diplomacy was not enough. Discussions being carried on with the Russians and with the French on behalf of the Russians proved unavailing. The Russian challenge in Korea threatened Japanese security, as did the Russian refusal to guarantee the integrity of China, the continued occupation of Manchuria, and the Russian reinforcement of its military position. The Japanese broke off negotiations on February 4, 1904.

Roosevelt understood all this and rejoiced in Tokyo's early successes in the war, passing off Russian failures as the result of the tsar's poor leadership.[11] Like most Americans he was jubilant over the Japanese surprise attack at Port Arthur on February 8 which opened the war. To Elihu Root he wrote, "Indeed the Japs showed themselves past masters in the practical application of David Harum's famous gloss on the 'Do unto others' injunction. They did it fust!"[12] Two days after Port Arthur he remarked in another private letter that the Russians had behaved badly in the Far East, especially toward the Japanese, toward whom they were grossly overbearing. He was thoroughly pleased with the Japanese victory at Port Arthur, for Japan was playing "our game."[13] He was apprehensive lest the Russians at the outset should defeat the Japanese on the sea, for then they might assume a well-nigh intolerable attitude toward the Americans. Minister Takahira, following the victory, stated that the United States should not fear a yellow peril; to

[11] TR to Hay, April 2, 1905, TR MSS.
[12] TR to Root, Feb. 16, 1904, Elihu Root MSS in the Library of Congress.
[13] TR to TR, Jr., Feb. 10, 1904, TR MSS.

which Secretary of State Hay wryly noted that he had never lost any sleep over it.[14]

This early Japanese victory set the pace for military operations throughout 1904. The Japanese had obvious advantages: location, superior forces and equipment, better intelligence work. The Russians had not been concerned about the possibility of war, and their planning showed it. The major part of the Russian military machine, and it must be noted the better part, was in the European section of the vast country, thousands of miles away. The Japanese knew this and realized timing was important. The attack on Port Arthur and the eventual destruction of the Russian fleet assured Japanese local control and permitted the army to begin operations. The army landed in Manchuria and began the campaign to push the Russians out of China. Victories followed at Yalu and Fenghuangcheng, and Japanese forces pushed on to Port Arthur to capture the Russian fortress. These military successes startled the world.

Perhaps equally important was the success of the wartime diplomacy pursued by the Island Empire, especially in its relations with the United States. Minister Takahira and his newly arrived colleague Baron Kaneko cultivated Roosevelt's like of the Japanese, and in their first meeting the president told Kaneko that a Japanese victory would prove a great blessing.[15] As early as March 1904 Roosevelt thanked Kaneko for two books, *Prince Gengi* and *Heroic Japan*. He believed no nation was worthy of respect unless its sons possessed loyalty and the courage, hardihood, and mental and physical address which made this loyalty effective; books which discussed the Samurai

[14] Hay Diary, Feb. 11, 1904, Hay MSS.

[15] Kaneko interview with TR, March 26, 1904, "Kaneko Dan to Bei Daitōryō to no kaiken shimatsu," Kaneko Reel MT804, Japanese Foreign Ministry Archives; see also Takahira to Komura, March 29, 1904 (#23), Kaneko Reel MT804, Japanese Foreign Ministry Archives.

spirit convinced him that Japan was such a nation.[16] He took wrestling lessons from Professor Y. Yamashita and was much impressed with the professor's skill and courage.[17] The president had Kaneko and Takahira to lunch at Oyster Bay in June, and at that time predicted a great future for the Japanese. He hoped Japan would take its place among the great civilized nations. He talked of Japan's special interest in the Yellow Sea, comparing it to America's in the Caribbean—a Japanese Monroe Doctrine. He hoped this interest would not mean a divided China and welcomed any part the Japanese took which would bring China along the road of civilization. His guests saw no reason for the Japanese to divide China, for Japan would have enough difficulty controlling Korea. Roosevelt warned the Japanese about forcing European mediation by demanding too much. He told the Japanese diplomats that a civilization such as they had developed entitled them to laugh at the accusation of being part of the yellow peril. When the conversation turned to the Philippines, the president's guests assured him that talk of hostile Japanese intentions there was nonsense. The Japanese closed the exchange by expressing fear that the Russians could not be trusted. This forced the envoys to question the value of peace negotiations.[18]

Roosevelt's private support of the Japanese continued through 1904, and the president wrote Secretary Hay that "the Japs have played our game because they have

[16] TR to Kaneko, March 31, 1904, and April 23, 1904, TR MSS.

[17] TR to Professor Y. Yamashita, April 23, 1904, TR MSS.

[18] Kaneko interview with TR, June 6, 1904, "Kaneko Dan to Bei Daitōryō to no kaiken shimatsu," Kaneko Reel MT804, Japanese Foreign Ministry Archives; see also Takahira to Komura, June 9, 1904 (#1959), and June 27, 1904 (#1986), and Komura to Takahira, June 13, 1904 (#14419), Telegram Series, Reels for 1904, Japanese Foreign Ministry Archives. Komura's comment about the interview was that he found it "very interesting." For Roosevelt's impression of the meeting, see TR to Spring Rice, June 13, 1904, TR MSS.

played the game of civilized mankind. People talk of the 'yellow peril,' and speak of the Mongol invasion of Europe. Why, the descendants of those very Mongols are serving under the banners of Russia, not under the banners of Japan." In September he told Hay what nonsense it was to speak of the Chinese and Japanese as of the same race.[19]

Takahira worked on Roosevelt's sympathy; in October 1904 Roosevelt thanked the minister for more books—*Japan's Beginning the Twentieth Century* and *The Ancestor Worship.* In mid-December the president told Kaneko he felt an affinity for the elements under the yellow skin, not under the Russian skin. Later Roosevelt acknowledged Takahira's Christmas present: another book—Mitford's *Tales of Old Japan.*[20]

How different was the presidential view of the Russians! At the outset of the war he had worried about a Russian victory, and he could not understand why the Russians were so unprepared.[21] He thought the great weakness of Russia was its government, a crushing despotism. "When I feel exasperated by the limitations upon preparedness and forethought which are imposed by democratic traditions," he wrote Spring Rice, "I can comfort myself by the extraordinary example of these very limitations which the autocratic government of Russia has itself furnished in this crisis." In another letter he noted that he liked the Russian people and believed in them, but that permanent good would not come until its people walked the path of freedom, civil liberty, and self-government. "Russia for a number of years has treated

[19] TR to Hay, July 26, 1904, and Sept. 2, 1904, TR MSS.

[20] TR to Takahira, Oct. 6, 1904, TR MSS; Kaneko interview with TR, Dec. 19, 1904, "Kaneko Dan to Bei Daitōryō to no kaiken shimatsu," Kaneko Reel MT804, Japanese Foreign Ministry Archives; and TR to Takahira, Dec. 27, 1904, TR MSS.

[21] TR to Reid, Feb. 11, 1904, Whitelaw Reid MSS in the Library of Congress.

the United States . . . almost as badly as she has treated Japan. Her diplomatists lied to us with brazen and contemptuous effrontery, and showed with cynical indifference their intentions to organize China against our interests."[22]

Secretary Hay encouraged Roosevelt's dislike of the Russians. The Russian government and especially Ambassador Cassini had disturbed Hay who told Joseph Choate how annoyed the Russians were because the United States would do nothing other than observe a strict neutrality. The Japanese, Hay noted, were sensible enough to be content with this.[23] For Cassini the secretary had special criticism. After the Russian had talked for an hour about American unfriendliness, Hay said the Japanese were more clever, for they spoke only of American friendliness. On the occasion of another visit by Cassini, Hay compared the Russian attitude as similar to a man who got into a quarrel on the street, then went home and beat his wife.[24] "Every time the Russians get a kick from the Japanese," he wrote the first secretary of the American embassy in St. Petersburg, "they turn and swear at us. If they would devote their energies to their real enemies and stop nagging and quarreling with their friends, it would be better for them."[25]

The president was wary of a sweeping Japanese victory, for that might puff the Japanese with pride and turn them against the United States. If the Japanese were to win, not only the Slavs but all the powers would have to reckon with a new force. The Japanese would have only one interest—the Far East—while other powers would have divided interests.[26] If the Japanese reorganized China there would be a shift of equilibrium concerning

22 TR to Spring Rice, March 19, 1904, and Dec. 27, 1904, TR MSS.

23 Hay to Joseph Choate, Feb. 27, 1904, Joseph Choate MSS in the Library of Congress.

24 Hay Diary, March 1, 1904, and June 3, 1904, Hay MSS.

25 Hay to Spencer Eddy, June 7, 1904, Hay MSS.

26 TR to Spring Rice, March 19, 1904, and June 13, 1904, TR MSS.

the white races. He told Takahira and Kaneko he hoped the Japanese would not claim more than what they started the war for. If the Japanese got a big head and entered into a general career of insolence and aggression it would be unpleasant. He wrote Spring Rice that a Japanese victory might mean a future struggle between Japan and the United States, though he hoped not.[27] He had become concerned with the display of Japanese might, especially the naval strength.

He had also learned there was a limit to his influence on the Tokyo government, through two incidents, both minor, of 1904. The first concerned newsmen who wanted to cover the war from the Japanese frontlines. They were forced to stay in Tokyo. The Japanese military, unlike the Russian, refused to allow them passage to the front. The reporters became restless as week after week went by. The president, realizing the value of press support, was concerned and advised Tokyo to let the journalists go to the front. The Japanese government persisted, and Prime Minister Taro Katsura told Griscom, through Foreign Minister Jutaro Komura, that the civil authorities could not interfere with the military conduct of the war. Later, apparently as a gesture to Roosevelt, the newsmen received permission to go to Manchuria, but they were kept from the frontlines and many returned to the United States with an unfavorable picture of Japan. The Japanese refusal to grant the necessary permissions surprised and puzzled the president.[28]

Much the same thing happened in the *Ryeshitelui*

[27] Kaneko interview with TR, June 6, 1904, "Kaneko Dan to Bei Daitōryō to no kaiken shimatsu," Kaneko Reel MT804, Japanese Foreign Ministry Archives; see also Takahira to Komura, June 9, 1904 (#1959), Telegram Series, Reels for 1904, Japanese Foreign Ministry Archives; and TR to Spring Rice, June 13, 1904, TR MSS.

[28] Griscom to Hay, April 28, 1904, Hay MSS; Griscom to Hay, June 30, 1904, SDA NA; and Hay to Roosevelt, July 21, 1904, Hay MSS.

incident. The *Ryeshitelui,* a Russian destroyer, took asylum in Chefoo, a neutral Chinese port, in August, following the Japanese defeat of the Russian Far Eastern fleet. The Japanese went into Chefoo, and captured and removed the ship. Roosevelt advised Takahira that Tokyo should return the ship to China. Tokyo refused. While the president admitted that the Japanese government was perhaps technically correct, he believed that Tokyo would "lose nothing but gain much by restoring that worthless boat to China." While no change occurred in the Japanese position on the *Ryeshitelui,* and Roosevelt again saw the stubbornness of the Tokyo government, the Japanese did learn from the incident. They were careful not to violate Chinese neutrality during the rest of the war.[29]

As Russian fortunes worsened, Roosevelt's—and Hay's—concern about the balance of power increased. Asking Meyer to accept the assignment in St. Petersburg, Roosevelt noted that the Far East needed watching. Tokyo would not show itself more altruistic than St. Petersburg or for that matter Berlin.[30] While the Japanese rulers had recognized Russia as their enemy, Roosevelt was not sure the Japanese people drew any distinction between Russians and other foreigners including Americans. He wondered if the Japanese did not lump Russians, English, Americans, and Germans "as white devils inferior to

29 Takahira to Komura, Aug. 17, 1904 (#18149), Takahira to Komura, Aug. 18, 1904 (#18171), Takahira to Komura, Aug. 20, 1904 (#18224), Telegram Series, Reels for 1904, Japanese Foreign Ministry Archives; and Griscom to Hay, Oct. 12, 1904, and Jan. 3, 1905, Hay MSS. There were other incidents in Japanese-American relations. A Russian cruiser, the *Lena,* entered San Francisco Bay, where American authorities, to the satisfaction of the Japanese, interned and disarmed the ship. This event occurred in September 1904. In October Tokyo settled a claim by the American Tobacco Company, and in November Prince Sadanaru visited the United States. All three of these events bettered relations between Washington and Tokyo, but could not offset the *Ryeshitelui* incident or the affair of the correspondents.

30 TR to Meyer, Dec. 26, 1904, Meyer MSS.

themselves" and plan "to take advantage of our various national jealousies, and beat us in turn."[31]

Thus by the end of 1904 Roosevelt had become concerned about Japanese domination of the Far East. Minister Tadasu Hayashi informed Tokyo from London that Roosevelt in an interview with a friend of the minister had spoken of his hope to see both the Russians and the Japanese exhausted by the war.[32] The military events of 1904 succeeded only in increasing Roosevelt's fear. The Japanese victories, the possible Russian collapse, the difficulties over correspondents and the *Ryeshitelui,* all brought about a change in the president's attitude.

There were other reasons why Roosevelt chose to mediate, apart from a Far Eastern balance of power. He was interested in mediating before anyone else had a chance to act as mediator, for he feared that intervention by an international congress would mean concessions to all powers at the expense of China.[33] He also feared mediation by any one of the European powers. He was concerned about possible German intervention, as were the Japanese. The aim of his policy toward Germany throughout the war was to keep the kaiser's friendship. He assured Wilhelm that the other neutral nations would not intervene, hoping to discourage any intervention thoughts that Berlin had. He also thought that the kaiser could help bring peace at the proper time by using Berlin's influence at St. Petersburg. To this purpose Roosevelt kept the Germans well informed about his activities, often seeking German opinion on favorable conditions.[34]

[31] TR to Spring Rice, Dec. 27, 1904, TR MSS.

[32] Hayashi to Komura, Dec. 5, 1904 (#22336), Telegram Series, Reels for 1904, Japanese Foreign Relations Archives.

[33] TR to Hay, March 30, 1905, TR MSS.

[34] For the correspondence between Washington and Berlin, see *Die Grosse Politik der Europäischen Kabinette, 1871-1914,* 40 vols. (Berlin, 1922-1927), esp. vol. 19.

By mediating, Roosevelt further believed he could guarantee victory for the Japanese government, preventing another triple intervention as in 1895. As early as May 1904 the president had told Hay that "we could hardly afford to allow a combination of R.G. & F. [Russia, Germany, and France] to step in and deprive Japan of the results of this war."[35] In January 1905 Hay recorded in his diary that the president was firm in the view that he would not permit Japan to be robbed a second time.[36] And Roosevelt wanted to stop a war between civilized powers–it was bad for the world. He frequently told Ambassador Jusserand that the French for this reason should advocate peace.

Did Roosevelt desire to mediate for his own personal advantage? Was he trying to take part in diplomacy to make himself better known? Minister Griscom noted that "to bring about peace between two warring powers is the dream of every president or ruler, and President Roosevelt was no exception. I received intimations from Washington that I should be on the lookout for the timely moment. It had to be carefully chosen; if the mediator offered his suggestion too soon, he ran the risk of a humiliating rebuff."[37] But this does not mean that Roosevelt had any personal ambitions as a peacemaker. In his most private letters there is no evidence. The main reason behind his desire to mediate the war was the Far Eastern balance of power.

When did the president decide he should bring peace between Russia and Japan in East Asia? It would seem that Roosevelt thought about taking the leading role in peacemaking even before the war began. The president

[35] Hay Diary, May 29, 1904, Hay MSS; and TR to Hay, July 26, 1904, TR MSS.
[36] Hay Diary, Jan. 1, 1905, Hay MSS.
[37] Lloyd Griscom, *Diplomatically Speaking* (Boston, 1940), 253.

had hated to see the outbreak of war. Before the Port Arthur attack he did his best to keep the two nations from each other's throats. The Japanese, realizing Roosevelt's sympathies, kept Washington posted of the negotiation in late 1903 and early 1904 with St. Petersburg. Tokyo explained the difficulties in dealing with the Russians and indicated that the situation might lead to war. In January 1904 Roosevelt asked Griscom if the Japanese would accept a mediation.[38] He persuaded the French ambassador in Washington to cable his government about mediation.[39] The initial Japanese decision to oppose all mediation ended this hope. Roosevelt wrote Oscar Straus that "unfortunately, Japan has notified us that she would regard any attempt at mediation as unfriendly because she insists that Russia is simply striving for delay and intends to take advantage of every delay to perfect her preparations." Next day he noted that he had done all he could.[40]

At this time he declared the American policy of strict neutrality, which he thought was the only way to build the framework from which he could ask for peace. Shortly after the fighting commenced, Roosevelt went beyond pronouncements of neutrality and issued a presidential order that all government officials remain neutral in speech and action in order to avoid offending either of the combatants.[41]

38 Komura to Takahira, Dec. 21 and 23, 1903, SDA NA; and Griscom to Secretary of State, Jan. 5, 1904, SDA NA.

39 Hay to TR, Jan. 5, 1904, Hay MSS; see also Hay Diary, Jan. 4, 5, and 11, 1904, Hay MSS.

40 TR to Straus, Feb. 9, 1904, Straus MSS; see also TR to Bishop Charles C. McCabe, Feb. 10, 1904, TR MSS; and Takahira to Komura, Jan. 12, 1904 (#175), Telegram Series, Reels for 1904, Japanese Foreign Ministry Archives. Takahira reported to Tokyo that he had told Hay that "mediation is not acceptable to Japan."

41 For Roosevelt's neutrality proclamation of Feb. 11, 1904, see *Papers Relating to the Foreign Relations of the United States; 1904* (Washington,

Roosevelt took a large step toward becoming the neutrals' leader, again in hope of peace. The German government had been urging him to support the neutrality of China. The kaiser wished an assurance that Russia, Japan, France, and England would not take Chinese territory; indeed it was he who set Roosevelt on the road of peacemaking. Three weeks before the surprise attack the president obtained private assurances from the Russian and Japanese representatives in Washington that in event of war both belligerents would respect Chinese neutrality.[42] Always suspecting a plot, the kaiser continued to press Roosevelt for guarantees from the warring nations to respect the neutrality of China. Through Speck von Sternburg, Berlin proposed that Roosevelt take the initiative to localize the conflict by calling for the neutrality of all Chinese territory that lay south of Talienwan, except the Liaotung peninsula. The Germans suggested that the neutrality be safeguarded by the major nonbelligerent powers. Despite some concern by experts on the Far East, especially Rockhill, Secretary Hay decided to proceed with the proposal. Hay and Roosevelt agreed to change the German suggestion so that there was no specific geographical neutrality line. Realizing that Manchuria would be the primary battleground, the Americans changed the limitation to respect China's administrative entity in all practical ways, adding that the belligerents should limit hostilities so that "undue excitement and disturbance of the Chinese people may be prevented and the least possible loss to the commerce and peaceful

---

D.C., 1905). The executive order issued by the president on March 10, 1904, to government officials, was enclosed in Hay to E. H. Conger in Peking, Dec. 1, 1904, SDA NA. See also Takahira to Komura, March 19, 1904 (#1863), Telegram Series, Reels for 1904, Japanese Foreign Ministry Archives.

[42] Hay Diary, Jan. 11, Feb. 16, 19, 21, and 22, 1904, Hay MSS.

intercourse of the world may be occasioned."[43] The proposal made no provision for safeguarding the neutral area and made no mention of Korea. Sent to all neutral powers as well as the belligerents, the note was ambiguous, perhaps intentionally so. It caused much confusion in the world capitals. Within days, however, the neutrals accepted. The Japanese agreed, on condition of Russian acceptance. Despite a Russian reply that seemed to call for consultation of the powers and excepted Manchuria from the guarantee, the president announced Russian agreement. Hay noted that Washington accepted "at once and finally the answer of Russia as responsive to our note."[44]

The president's peace efforts continued throughout 1904, without success. Concern for the power balance and desire for peace stood out, privately as well as in public: "And I am no less sincere in my hope that the area of the war will be as limited as much as possible, and that it will be brought to a close with as little loss to either combatant as is possible."[45] On many occasions he met Takahira, urging a good military position, at the same time trying to learn Japan's terms. He discovered

[43] Rockhill to TR, and Memo by Rockhill, both Feb. 6, 1904, TR MSS; Hay Diary, Feb. 7 and 8, 1904, Hay MSS; and circular note of TR to Japan, Russia, Germany, England, and France, as well as other nations, Feb. 8 and 10, 1904, SDA NA.

[44] Komura to Takahira, Feb. 11, 1904 (#2025), and Komura to Hayashi, Feb. 13, 1904 (#1636), Telegram Series, Reels for 1904, Japanese Foreign Ministry Archives; Komura to Griscom, Feb. 13, 1904, and Griscom to Secretary of State, Feb. 13, 1904, SDA NA; see also Robert McCormick to Secretary of State, Feb. 14, 17, and 19, 1904, SDA NA; and Hay Diary, Feb. 19 and 21, 1904, Hay MSS. Neither the president nor Hay thought they could gain the neutrality of Manchuria. A related question has to do with Manchuria after the war. Was Manchuria included in the call to preserve the territorial integrity of China? Washington probably included Manchuria, but the Americans were not willing to risk defeat of the proposal on such a demand. Throughout the war, Roosevelt did call for the restoration of Manchuria to China.

[45] TR to Spring Rice, March 19, 1904, TR MSS.

that the Japanese opposed mediation because it would help the Russians. He soothed the Japanese who protested Russian ships in neutral ports. And in June Roosevelt expressed his ideas on peacemaking to his Japanese confidants. He told Takahira and Kaneko that though the time had not yet arrived he would try to perform good offices for the Japanese. To help bring about such a situation he hoped that Tokyo would not expect excessive conditions and indicated that the Japanese should not go north of Mukden.[46] Roosevelt bothered the Russian ambassador enough that Secretary Hay reported Cassini's throwing a pink fit at any reference of peace.[47] The president had to admit that the Russians formally had notified the powers that they would resent any attempt at mediation.[48]

The announced leader of the neutrals likewise talked with Speck von Sternburg about American aims in the Far East and tried to enlist the kaiser's help. In one of these talks the president described suitable peace terms. Strength of the belligerents should be as equal as possible—he did not want a serious deterioration of Russian Far Eastern power. Contested areas would be as before; Japan could have Korea, guaranteeing interests of the major powers there, but must not establish itself in China. America would recognize Russian dominance in Manchuria, although the Russians would have to give up Port Arthur. In August in another conversation with the ambassador he made proposals to the kaiser: he proposed that Manchuria be placed under a Chinese viceroy appointed by Germany, with neutrality jointly guaranteed by the great powers;

46 Kaneko interview with TR, June 6, 1904, "Kaneko Dan to Bei Daitōryō to no kaiken shimatsu," Kaneko Reel MT804, Japanese Ministry Archives.

47 Hay to Henry White, May 5, and Nov. 11, 1904, Hay MSS.

48 TR to Bishop McCabe, Sept. 1, 1904, TR MSS.

if Japanese successes continued, there could not be another coalition of the powers as in 1895. Speck von Sternburg thought these terms would have the kaiser's support. When this proposal arrived in Berlin, Bülow told the German ruler that Roosevelt was sincere and had no hostile intent.[49]

England, Roosevelt thought, had no man he could deal with; he did not think much of Lansdowne. He wondered how he was to deal with Ambassador Durand. With the French (though not personally with Jusserand) he was in similar position. That left only the Germans, and he told Speck von Sternburg that the only man he understood and who understood him was the kaiser.[50]

But the kaiser, involved in an intrigue with his imperial cousin the tsar, would not assist the president. Throughout 1904 the kaiser pressed the tsar to continue the war; "there is no doubt to me that you will and must win in the long run, but it will cost both money and many men."[51] Privately the German ruler believed the Russians would rally and neutralize the Japanese. Russia might become weakened by the war and would become more involved in the Far East—what the kaiser wanted.[52] So he warned Nicholas. He was sure the British would renew efforts to make proposals about mediation: such was the special mission of the British ambassador in St. Petersburg, Charles

[49] Hermann Speck von Sternburg to Bülow, May 9, 1904 (#5994), *Die Grosse Politik der Europäischen Kabinette,* vol. 19, pt. 1; and Bülow to Wilhelm II, Aug. 31, 1904, Whyte, *Letters of Prince von Bülow.* The Germans were unwilling to have their hands tied, as is seen in Bülow to the kaiser, Aug. 31, 1904, *Die Grosse Politik der Europäischen Kabinette,* vol. 19, pt. 2, but Berlin kept on friendly terms with Washington.

[50] Speck von Sternburg to Bülow, Sept. 27, 1904 (#6266), *Die Grosse Politik der Europäischen Kabinette,* vol. 19, pt. 1.

[51] Kaiser Wilhelm to Nicholas, Aug. 19, 1904, Levine, *Letters from the Kaiser to the Czar;* von Gerlach, *Briefe und Telegramme Wilhelms II an Nikolaus II—1894-1914;* Pokrovsky, *Perepiska Vilgelma vtorogo s Nikolaem vtorym.*

[52] Memorandum of Bülow, Jan. 16, 1904, and Bülow to Wilhelm II, Feb. 26, 1904, Whyte, *Letters of Prince von Bülow.*

Hardinge. The kaiser added surprisingly that he would be available to the tsar should mediation seem advisable. Wilhelm privately hoped he could take Russia out of the French alliance; talk of a possible Anglo-French entente had started. The kaiser pointed out to the tsar that "the row [*sic*] steel material [for Japan] is being produced in France (Greuzot)—your Ally!—and to be finished in Japan. To be delivered to Tientsin in May next."[53] The Anglo-French entente proved that the French had abandoned the Russians. In June 1904 he wrote that after many hints and allusions he found out what he always feared—the Anglo-French agreement had one main purpose, to stop the French from helping the Russians. As months passed his fear of German encirclement grew and so did his charges against the French. In October he reported to Nicholas: "I positively know that as far back as December last the French Minister of Finance [Maurice] Rouvier from his own accord told the Financial Agent of another Power, that on no account whatever would France join you in a Russo-Japanese war, even if England should take sides with Japan."[54] He was not able to convince the Russians. If he concluded a German-Russian commercial treaty on July 28, 1904, perhaps a prelude to the famous imperial meeting at Björkö in 1905, nothing came of the effort.

In 1904 the war was going well for the Japanese—one success after another—but a peace party in the summer led by Marquis Ito pressed the government to stop the expensive war. Ito's counterpart in St. Petersburg, Count

[53] Kaiser Wilhelm to Nicholas, Feb. 11, 1904, and June 6, 1904, Levine, *Letters from the Kaiser to the Czar;* von Gerlach, *Briefe und Telegramme Wilhelms II an Nikolaus II—1894-1914;* Pokrovsky, *Perepiska Vilgelma vtorogo s Nikolaem vtorym.*

[54] Kaiser Wilhelm to Nicholas, Oct. 30, 1904, Levine, *Letters from the Kaiser to the Czar;* von Gerlach, *Briefe und Telegramme Wilhelms II an Nikolaus II—1894-1914;* Pokrovsky, *Perepiska Vilgelma vtorogo s Nikolaem vtorym.*

Sergei Witte, led a formidable group of statesmen and bankers who deplored the war. Witte sought an interview with the Japanese minister in London, Hayashi, who for a while became the soul of these peace talks. Negotiation dragged through June and ended on July 28 with the assassination of the Russian minister of the interior, Count V. K. Plehve. The Japanese would welcome peace, Hayashi wrote, and would cultivate friendship with its present enemy after the conclusion of peace. The proposal for peace had to come from the power that caused the war.[55]

The French also made proposals, the most serious when the ambassador in St. Petersburg, Maurice Bompard, acting on instruction from Delcassé, visited Minister Motono in Paris and extended his good offices. After consulting Tokyo, Motono rejected them, saying the Japanese opposed all intervention of a third power.[56]

How far from peace the belligerents were in 1904 appears in British dispatches describing the Russian and Japanese attitudes toward a cessation of hostilities. In a conversation with Hardinge in St. Petersburg, Witte said victory would be necessary. He admitted that much would depend on whether the war ended early in a succession of victories, or after great sacrifices of men and material. In any case, he said, opinion was unanimous that Japan had to be crippled and Russian predominance on the Pacific Coast assured. This meant Russian absorption of Manchuria and Korea. Just as the Treaty of Paris after the Crimean War prevented Russia from having a fleet on the Black Sea, Witte continued, Japan should have no fleet on the Yellow Sea, and in addition to Port Arthur the Russians had to control the mouth of the

[55] A. M. Pooley, *Secret Memoirs of Baron Tadasu Hayashi* (New York, 1915), 232-34.

[56] Maurice Bompard, *Mon Ambassade en Russie, 1903-1908* (Paris, 1937), 94-95.

Yalu and command the Korean straits. These were the Russians' terms.[57]

Marquis Ito pointed out in Tokyo that the only route to lasting peace lay in internationalization of the Trans-Siberian from the point where it entered Chinese territory. Japan had been driven to war by sheer fear of aggression, Ito said, when it saw that even Korea was not escaping Russian encroachments. The Japanese neither wanted Manchuria nor were strong enough to maintain large garrisons on the remote borders of that province. They would respect the integrity of China. Their position, Ito concluded, was that "it was unprofitable for any country to endeavor to go beyond those limits which appear to have been set by nature to its powers: to do so was to open a source of weakness, and of this Russia was, he thought, an example."[58]

Meanwhile life went on in the United States. Americans had read in their newspapers of the war and the smashing Japanese victories—rather, such information appeared in their papers; probably few read it. Their minds were far from East Asia. They were perhaps aware that many world officials, including their own president, desired peace. They found more interesting the fashion, sports, and comic sections of the papers. The president was busy with domestic matters, listening to the reaction to Booker T. Washington's visit to the White House. He was also trying to get himself elected as president, in opposition to a New York banker, the Democratic party's candidate Alton B. Parker.

[57] Charles Hardinge to Lord Lansdowne, June 30, 1904 (#3), *British Documents on the Origins of the War, 1898-1914,* 11 vols. (London, 1926-1938), IV: see also Bülow's report of a conversation he had with Sergei Witte, in Bülow to Kaiser Wilhelm, June 15, 1904, Whyte, *Letters of Prince von Bülow.*

[58] Memorandum to Mr. T. B. Hohler, enclosed in Claude MacDonald to Lansdowne, Nov. 22, 1904 (#57), *British Documents on the Origins of the War, 1898-1914,* IV.

Chapter Three

THE FIRST STEP TO PEACE

So women with babes at their bosoms
Gazed out o'er the furrows untilled,
Through the haze resting red like the blood that was shed
In a far-away struggle unwilled.
And eyes that are swollen and anguished
Uplifted in silent appeal;
"O God of the Poor, does thy mercy endure
When thy monarchs know naught but of steel?"[1]

AFTER HIS ELECTION in late 1904 Theodore Roosevelt worked to end the Russo-Japanese War. He was president in his own right. His previous status had bothered him; he mentioned it in letters and talks; he had delayed much of what he wanted to do as president. He could now act to end a war still removed from the minds of his countrymen but close to the destiny of his country.

From the beginning of 1905 until the battle of Tsushima, Roosevelt's diplomacy was similar to the frustrating months of 1904, only more complicated and active. Many people saw the need for peace but did not know how to achieve it. The second phase of his negotiation came after Tsushima, May 27-28, 1905, for the Russians were losing the war and the monarchy seemed on the verge of collapse.

The surrender of the fortress of Port Arthur, the first major Russian land disaster, occurred on New Year's day, 1905—not a promising sign for the Russian monarchy. Under attack for many months, the Russians under General A. M. Stessel capitulated and the Japanese took 24,369 prisoners. Port Arthur was the key to Russian coastal strength. It was, of course, a symbol and made easier the Japanese attempts to borrow money in the world financial centers. The Japanese had gained revenge for their humiliation of 1895. Many people now expected the St. Petersburg government to sue for peace, especially as the internal situation in Russia was unsettled. The British minister in Tokyo, Claude MacDonald, reported, "In certain usually well-informed circles an idea seems to be prevalent that now that Port Arthur has fallen peace is within measurable distance."[2] Instead the diplomacy of 1905 became more complex and for a time it appeared that the war might expand to include some of the neutral powers.

The European nations, especially Germany, were beginning to use the Far Eastern situation to manipulate the European balance of power. The Germans wished the open door in the Orient and to win Russia from France and England. The kaiser's fear of Russia in Europe made him wish the Russians weakened, while at the same time he felt sympathy for a fellow autocrat, especially one he could dominate. The German ruler learned that the French alone knew the Russians' conditions for peace. He complained to his cousin that Berlin should learn of the Russian terms directly from St. Petersburg.[3] Wilhelm also began to tell President Roosevelt of French plans against the integrity of China and the open door; the French purpose, he said, was to convince the belligerents that peace was impossible without compensation to the

[1] New York *Times,* May 18, 1905.

[2] MacDonald to Lansdowne, Jan. 12, 1905 (#60), *British Documents on the Origins of the War, 1898-1914,* 11 vols. (London, 1926-1938), IV.

[3] Wilhelm to Nicholas, Jan. 2, 1905, I. D. Levine, ed., *Letters from the Kaiser to the Czar* (New York, 1920); Hellmuth von Gerlach, ed., *Briefe und Telegramme Wilhelms II an Nikolaus II—1894-1914* (Berlin, 1920); M. N. Pokrovsky, ed., *Perepiska Vilgelma vtorogo s Nikolaem vtorym* (Moscow, 1923).

neutral powers; the kaiser wondered if Roosevelt would ask the powers interested in the Far East not to take territory or other compensation in China or elsewhere for services rendered to the belligerents. Roosevelt thanked the emperor for his assurance of disinterest in territorial acquisitions.[4] He knew he would need Wilhelm's help to get the Russians to agree to peace ("Evidently the Emperor is really alarmed about France. . . . You notice how he keeps repeating the phrase, 'the integrity of China' ").[5] Secretary Hay sent a diplomatic circular calling for the neutral nations to renounce territorial ambitions in China. All the nations accepted the American proposal.[6]

Behind the scenes the kaiser campaigned against peace in letters to Nicholas in early 1905. He wrote that the fall of Port Arthur created a sensation. All Germans felt deep sympathy for the valiant generals and the brave diminishing band of heroes. He warned of an armistice and even peace.[7]

Adding to Roosevelt's problems was a Russian charge that the Chinese had violated neutrality by helping the Japanese. Ambassador Cassini recalled that the Russian government "guided by humane considerations" had agreed "to the proposition of the Washington Cabinet, having in view the localization of the military operations and the neutralization of the Chinese territory." This decision St. Petersburg had made known by a circular note of February 1904. Although eleven months of war demonstrated that the Chinese were neither capable nor desirous

[4] Baron Hilmar von dem Bussche-Haddenhausen to TR, Jan. 5, 1905, and TR to Speck von Sternburg, Jan. 10 and 12, 1905, TR MSS.

[5] TR to Hay, Jan. 12, 1905, TR MSS.

[6] Hay to the major neutral nations, Jan. 13, 1905, SDA NA.

[7] Wilhelm to Nicholas, Jan. 2, 1905, Levine, *Letters from the Kaiser to the Czar;* von Gerlach, *Briefe und Telegramme Wilhelms II an Nikolaus II—1894-1914;* Pokrovsky, *Perepiska Vilgelma vtorogo s Nikolaem vtorym.*

of living up to their pledges, Cassini reported that the Chinese were making serious military preparations. The Russian government, he said, might not continue to guarantee China's neutrality.[8] Roosevelt advised Hay to protest any violation of Chinese neutrality. Hay during one of Cassini's frequent visits told of China's declarations of neutrality and noted that he had communicated the Russian complaint to the minister in China and instructed him to make known to the foreign office in Peking the earnest hope of the President that "China will scrupulously observe neutral obligations, any departure from which would seriously embarrass not only China, but also the powers interested in limiting the area of hostilities."[9] Cassini thanked Hay for the assistance, maintaining that no evidence supported Chinese denials.[10]

Roosevelt at this time was completing his diplomatic network by moving Meyer to St. Petersburg, from Rome. Meyer had accepted the Russian assignment by telegraphing: "Letter received today; appreciate the compliment; accept with pleasure." In his diary he noted that the president was very complimentary, saying he wanted a man not afraid to work yet who could mingle with his colleagues and the Russian nobility.[11] Only after Meyer arrived in April could Roosevelt deal easily with both belligerents.

As reports came in of Father George Gapon's unfortunate march on the Winter Palace and the beginnings of the Russian revolution of 1905, the president increasingly desired peace. Meyer had written from Rome that

[8] Arturo Cassini to Hay, Jan. 13, 1905, SDA NA.

[9] TR to Hay, Jan. 16, 1905, TR MSS; and Francis Loomis (assistant secretary of state) to John Gardner Coolidge (Chargé in Peking), Jan. 14, 1905, SDA NA; see also Waiwu Pu to Chinese Minister in Washington, Jan. 21, 1905, and Hay to Cassini, Jan. 17, 1905, SDA NA.

[10] Cassini to Hay, Jan. 18, 1905, SDA NA.

[11] Meyer to TR, Jan. 20, 1905, TR MSS; and Meyer Diary, Jan. 20, 1905, Meyer MSS LC.

revolution was astir throughout Russia. The ambassador felt that a revolution could not succeed because of geographical conditions, lack of ammunition, finances, and leadership, but that any uprising would strengthen the Japanese military position.[12] The Russian peace party became vocal. Witte wrote the tsar that the only rational way out was to open negotiations on peace. The Russian admitted that it was painful to begin negotiations and that it would be necessary to accept only those conditions which would safeguard the imperial power.[13] The women of Moscow addressed an appeal to the empress, as a woman and a mother: hearts that are breaking "cannot remain silent." They promised help in leading the country on the road to greatness, should the emperor decide on peace.[14]

Even the kaiser's letters to the tsar began to talk of peace. Wilhelm warned that Russian opinion considered the tsar responsible for the war and that want of preparation was his fault. He told Nicholas that responsibility was a serious thing for a ruler but not overwhelming when the people supported the war. He suggested that Nicholas try to win back popularity, and making peace seemed the sure way.[15]

But the Japanese by the end of January 1905 did not believe peace was at hand. Komura told the British

[12] Meyer to TR, Jan. 28, 1905, TR MSS.

[13] Witte to Tsar Nicholas, March 13, 1905, *Sbornik diplomaticheskikh dokumentov kasaiushchikhsia peregovorov mezhdu Rossieiu i Iaponieiu o zakliuchenii mirnago dogovora 24 maia-3 oktiabria* [Collection of Diplomatic Documents Concerning Negotiations Between Russia and Japan About the Conclusion of the Peace Treaty May 24-October 3] (St. Petersburg, 1906); hereafter cited as *Sbornik diplomaticheskikh dokumentov.*

[14] *The Advocate of Peace,* LXVII (1905), 53, and *The Arbitrator,* CCCXXXV (1905), 195, Peace Collection in the Swarthmore College Library.

[15] Wilhelm to Nicholas, Feb. 21, 1905, Levine, *Letters from the Kaiser to the Czar;* von Gerlach, *Briefe und Telegramme Wilhelms II an Nikolaus II—1894-1914;* Pokrovsky, *Perepiska Vilgelma vtorogo s Nikolaem vtorym.*

minister that until the Japanese won a victory at Mukden the Russian government, he thought, would not make any overtures. The Japanese expected large-scale hostilities.[16] The president saw Kaneko on January 7 and 8, 1905, telling him that the neutrals were moving toward favor of his country. These talks, held at ten o'clock in the evening to avoid publicity, contained the same appeal: Japan should make peace while in a strong military position.[17] Sometime in January, Roosevelt intimated he again was ready to extend good offices: "I privately and unofficially advised the Russian Government, and afterwards repeated the advice indirectly through the French." He told the Russians that if they continued the war they could not count on favorable terms.[18] The president meanwhile was having troubles with China, the government of which had announced early in 1904 that it would not renew the immigration treaty signed with the United States ten years before—a treaty the Chinese, with good reason, considered humiliating. In December 1904 the Chinese canceled the concession of the American China Development Company to build the Canton-Hankow Railway. In early 1905 a boycott of American goods began. Businessmen besieged Roosevelt with demands for protection.

The Japanese at Mukden on March 10, following occupation of Port Arthur in January, won a great victory. For weeks the armies had fought—300,000 Japanese against 310,000 Russians. But in Japan war resources were almost

16 MacDonald to Lansdowne, Jan. 12, 1905 (#60), *British Documents on the Origins of the War, 1898-1914,* IV.

17 Kaneko interview with TR, Jan. 7, 1905, "Kaneko Dan to Bei Daitōryō to no kaiken shimatsu," Kaneko Reel MT804, Japanese Foreign Ministry Archives.

18 TR to George Otto Trevelyan, March 9, 1905, TR MSS. There is no other record of these warnings by Roosevelt to the Russians and the French and therefore there remains some doubt that anything other than admonitions were given to the ambassadors of these countries.

exhausted and the government under financial pressure, so intense that Takahira had talked to Secretary Hay about soliciting the good offices of Italy. Hay warned the Japanese minister to be careful about entanglements.[19] On March 9—the day before the surrender at Mukden—Roosevelt received word that Japan might shortly ask him to be peacemaker. Griscom had learned at a dinner party of the military's desire for peace; the minister of war, Masatake Terauchi, told him it was time for the fighting to stop. Unsure whether this was an official peace feeler, Griscom talked to an American working for the Japanese Foreign Ministry, Henry Denison, and then found out from Komura that Terauchi had expressed personal views. In fact Komura stated that Tokyo had detailed peace terms but would only discuss them if the Japanese government was sure the initiation had come from St. Petersburg. Komura concluded by expressing doubt that the Russians would be willing to talk until the Baltic fleet's fate was settled. Still, Griscom telegraphed Washington that Tokyo planned to ask Roosevelt to mediate at the proper time. Roosevelt was afraid that Griscom had put him forward as mediator, and the president replied that he would gain gratification to be of use in such an important event but would not offer his services if any other agency seemed more practical.[20] The Japanese after Mukden had announced they would welcome peace, but the Russians would have to make the first move.[21] Komura told MacDonald that the tsar and court had determined to continue the war. Japan entered into the war, Komura concluded, with full knowledge that it would be a long business and was quite prepared to

19 Hay Diary, Feb. 4, 1905, Hay MSS.

20 Griscom to Hay, March 9, 10, 13, and 15, 1905, and Hay to Griscom, March 11, 1905, SDA NA; Hay Diary, March 11, 1905, Hay MSS; and Takahira to Hay, March 15, 1905, Hay MSS.

21 Takahira to Hay, March 15, 1905, Hay MSS.

fight to the end. Mediation "would be little short of madness, for the War Party in Russia would at once look upon it as a sign of weakness, and be strengthened in their resolve to continue the war."[22]

The president met several times with Takahira, seeking to learn Japan's terms. A curtain of reticence descended: Tokyo refused publicly to disclose its position in regard to an indemnity and other demands.[23] In letters to the ailing secretary of state, dated March 30 and April 2, Roosevelt wrote that Cassini as well as Takahira, and also Durand, Jusserand, and Speck von Sternburg, had spoken about peace negotiations. Cassini told the president, doubtless under instruction, that the Russians would like peace on honorable terms, but that not for a moment could they consider an indemnity. Roosevelt pointed out to the ambassador that Japan's terms would be less severe before the Japanese had obtained Russian territory. "Did you ever know anything more pitiable than the condition of the Russian despotism in this year of grace," Roosevelt sighed to Hay in frustration, "the Czar is a preposterous little creature as the absolute autocrat of 150,000,000 people. He has been unable to make war, and he is now unable to make peace."[24]

The president left Washington on April 3 for a combined political and vacation trip to the west. He authorized Secretary of War Taft to "sit on the lid." Taft had attended one of the president's late evening sessions with Kaneko on March 20, 1905, when Roosevelt told of his planned bear hunt, saying to the Japanese representative that if anything came up Taft was to be an intermediary. Taft said Roosevelt's success would be a good sign for the Japanese fleet at the expected clash with the Russian

22 MacDonald to Lansdowne, March 24, 1905 (#65), *British Documents on the Origins of the War, 1898-1914*, IV.

23 TR to Hay, March 30, and April 2, 1905, TR MSS.

24 *Ibid.*

Baltic squadron then in route to the Far East. Roosevelt promised to return if he were needed.[25]

At this juncture there was one more attempt to help the Russians. At a diplomatic reception Delcassé told the Japanese minister in Paris he could bring the Japanese and Russians together should Tokyo waive certain conditions inadmissible by Russia. Delcassé explained that cession of Russian territory or payment of indemnity was humiliating. He favored direct negotiation. Minister Motono reported this information to Tokyo and in an attempt to find out whether this was a peace feeler from St. Petersburg, shortly asked the foreign minister if the Russians were sincere. Delcassé entertained, he replied, a conviction of Russia's desire for peace. Motono said later the Japanese government was pleased to know that France favored direct negotiation, but that his country refused mediation because in violation of the principle of direct negotiation the Japanese were asked to agree to conditions.[26]

At this time the Japanese publicly put the issue to Roosevelt. In a special cabinet meeting on April 8, the Japanese decided to take steps to bring about a satisfactory peace. In an interview with Taft, telegraphed immediately to Roosevelt on his hunt, Takahira said the French were attempting to mediate, asking moderate terms, and the Japanese would refuse all but direct negotiation. Takahira said his government felt that good offices might bring the belligerents together, and expressed his preference for Roosevelt by asking what steps

[25] Kaneko interview with TR and William Howard Taft, March 20, 1905, "Kaneko Dan to Bei Daitōryō to no kaiken shimatsu," Kaneko Reel MT804, Japanese Foreign Ministry Archives.

[26] Hayashi to Komura, April 3, 1905 (#2816), Telegram Series, Reels for 1905, Japanese Foreign Ministry Archives; Lansdowne to MacDonald, April 19, 1905 (#68), *British Documents on the Origins of the War, 1898-1914,* IV; and B. F. Barnes (assistant secretary of state) to William Loeb, April 18, 1905, TR MSS.

should be taken.[27] Even while he was in the Far West, ending the Russo-Japanese War was foremost in the president's mind, notwithstanding his Texas reunion with the Roughriders, the foot races in his camp in Oklahoma, and finally his successful bear hunt which led Takahira to remark, "I notice the President has got two bears. We would be satisfied with one!"[28]

THE SAGA of the voyage of the fleet around the world began on August 24, 1904, when the Russians decided to send the ill-prepared ships to offset Japanese naval strength in the Far East. The fleet departed in mid-October, was involved a week later in the famous Dogger Bank incident —in which Russian ships shelled British fishing vessels mistaken for Japanese torpedo boats, almost causing a war between Russia and Great Britain—and then headed south for the trip around Africa. Under the command of Rear Admiral Zinovii Rozhdestvensky, the fleet was the last hope for victory. Meyer, now in St. Petersburg, recorded in his diary that Rozhdestvensky's fleet had raised the spirits of the war party. On instruction of the president he told the tsar that Roosevelt gladly would use good offices toward an honorable and lasting peace. Nicholas looked embarrassed, saying he was glad to hear it, but turned the conversation. Throughout the talk, Meyer wrote, the empress stood near, never taking her eyes off the tsar.[29] Meyer's reports said internal conditions were bad. "The ship of state continues to drift without a definite course," he noted, "and no one in reality at the helm. While the obstacles that it meets are as yet in-

27 Barnes to Loeb, April 18, 1905, TR MSS.
28 John Callan O'Laughlin to TR, April 23, 1905, TR MSS.
29 Meyer Diary, April 16, 1905, Meyer MSS LC; State Department to Meyer, March 27, 1905, SDA NA; and Meyer to TR, April 13, 1905, TR MSS.

sufficient to arrest its own momentum, should Rojestvensky's fleet be destroyed and another victory gained in Manchuria by Japan, it would be difficult, with the astounding administrative incoherence and the excited condition of the public mind, to foretell coming events."[30] The government was in a comatose state, awaiting the naval conflict and the next battle near Harbin.[31]

With the fleet's destruction on May 27-28—an epic event in world history (the Pearl Harbor attack fleet of December 1941 would fly the 1905 command flag from the masthead of the leading carrier)—every Japanese took heart, and Kaneko closed his letter to Roosevelt announcing the success with a triumphant "banzai!!!"[32] The Japanese victory was complete. Vice Admiral Heihachiro Togo had planned carefully and caught the Russian fleet in the Straits of Tsushima. Almost all the Russian ships became casualties and even Rozhdestvensky was captured.

Three days after Tsushima, Komura instructed Takahira that Tokyo expected St. Petersburg to turn to peace. The Japanese government, Takahira was to say, still adhered to the conviction that peace negotiations, when they came, were to be conducted directly and exclusively between the belligerents. Friendly assistance of a neutral was essential to bring them together, and Takahira was to ask Roosevelt "directly and entirely of his own motion and initiative to invite the two belligerents to come together for the purpose of direct negotiation." The Japanese left procedure to the president.[33]

Here, at last, after Tsushima, was the opportunity Roosevelt had been awaiting. While the Japanese note

[30] Meyer to TR, April 24, 1905, TR MSS.

[31] Meyer to Henry Cabot Lodge, May 6, 1905, Henry Cabot Lodge MSS in the Massachusetts Historical Society.

[32] Kaneko to TR, May 30, 1905, and TR to Kaneko, May 31, 1905, TR MSS.

[33] Takahira to Loeb, May 31, 1905, TR MSS.

reminded him of a request for contributions sent by campaign committees to officeholders in which they asked for a voluntary contribution of 10 percent, he was ready to act.[34] He urged Cassini to get an agreement to a conference. The ambassador replied with "his usual rigmarole, to the effect that Russia was fighting the battles of the white race . . . that Russia was too great to admit defeat, and so forth." The president made Cassini promise to convey his views to St. Petersburg. Cassini soon showed up with a note that his government neither asked for peace nor wanted mediation.[35] One can almost sense the president's rage at Cassini, as the Russian stood there denying that his country needed peace. "Oh Lord! I have been going nearly mad in the effort to get Russia and Japan together." The more he saw of the tsar, the kaiser, and the mikado the more content he was with democracy, even if he had to include the American newspapers as one of its assets. To Roosevelt, Russia seemed corrupt, treacherous and shifty, and incompetent.[36]

To make sure his views were heard by the tsar, Roosevelt instructed Meyer to "call on His Majesty the Czar and say that he does so by personal direction of the President to urge upon His Majesty the desirability of his consenting to the request of the President to have representatives of Russia meet with representatives of Japan to confer as to whether peace can not now be made." Meyer was to inform Nicholas that the president was speaking for what was best for Russia, that he believed the present contest hopeless, and that to continue

[34] TR to Lodge, June 16, 1905, Lodge MSS.

[35] TR to Lodge, June 16, 1905, Lodge MSS; Cassini to Count Vladimir Lamsdorff, June 4, 1905 (#2), *Sbornik diplomaticheskikh dokumentov;* and Lamsdorff to Cassini, June 6, 1905, in Cassini to TR, June 6, 1905, TR MSS.

[36] TR to Lodge, June 16, 1905, Lodge MSS; and TR to Reid, June 30, 1905, TR MSS.

could only end in loss of all Russian possessions in East Asia. Direct negotiation between Russian and Japanese plenipotentiaries, without an intermediary, was necessary. If Russia would consent to such a meeting, Meyer was to tell the tsar, the president would try to get Japan's consent, acting on his own initiative and not saying Russia had agreed. Nothing would be public until the Japanese accepted: then the president would ask each power to agree to a meeting.[37] Anxious to get agreement, Roosevelt communicated the dispatch to Speck von Sternburg, Jusserand, and H. J. O'Beirne, the latter being the first secretary of the British embassy.[38] He believed the kaiser would back it up, and hoped Delcassé would too. He expected little aid from the British.[39]

The president had reached a commanding position. Meyer hastened to the Foreign Office to ask for an audience with the tsar, and was fortunate enough to catch Count Lamsdorff leaving to board the train for Tsarskoe Selo. Lamsdorff was discouraging about an audience before two or three days. Meyer offered to go down that afternoon or evening, and the foreign minister replied, "You must realize that every hour of the Emperor's time is taken up with engagements for several days, and tomorrow will be Her Majesty's birthday; there will also be a family breakfast in the Palace, and His Majesty has never granted an audience on that day." Meyer would not give up, and asked Lamsdorff to tell Nicholas that the president wished Meyer to lay before His Majesty a proposition received that morning by cable. Lamsdorff

[37] TR to Meyer, June 5, 1905, Meyer MSS and (#1), *Sbornik diplomaticheskikh dokumentov.*

[38] TR to Speck von Sternburg, Jusserand, O'Beirne, June 5, 1905, TR MSS.

[39] Roosevelt misunderstood the British motives, for the British were willing to aid him early in 1905. The best statement of the British position is in Ian Nish, *The Anglo-Japanese Alliance* (London, 1966).

said Meyer would have a reply before 5:00 P.M. The ambassador returned home. At last, as he recorded in his diary, "at 4[45] I recd. word that his majesty would grant me an audience at 2 o ck on Wed which the day [*sic*] of the Empress birthday—when audience have never been granted!!"[40]

He left St. Petersburg at 1:00 P.M. the next day, in a private train car, for the short trip to Tsarskoe Selo. He thought the garden of the palace very pretty with lilacs in full bloom. He was escorted directly to the room adjoining Nicholas's study; promptly at two o'clock the door of the study opened and the tsar came forward to meet Meyer. The visit lasted about an hour. Pointing out that it was of utmost importance that war should cease, Meyer asked Nicholas if Russia would consent to meet the Japanese, without intermediaries, should the president extend such an invitation. The tsar said it was difficult, assuring the ambassador he was convinced his people did not desire peace at any price and would support him in war. Meyer pointed out the futility of the war, its unpopularity, the threat of revolution. Even the emperor of Germany was in favor of peace. Nicholas admitted that, for he had just received a letter from Wilhelm.[41] For a while there was silence. At last the tsar said, "If it will be absolutely secret as to my decision, should Japan decline, or until she gives her consent, I will now consent to your President's plan that we [Russia and Japan] have a meeting *without intermediaries* in order to see if we can make peace." In making this decision without consulting any advisers, Nicholas told Meyer that the ambassador had come at a psychological moment: as yet no foot

[40] Meyer to TR, June 9, 1905, TR MSS; and Meyer Diary, June 6, 1905, Meyer MSS LC.

[41] Wilhelm to Nicholas, June 3, 1905, Levine, *Letters from the Kaiser to the Czar;* von Gerlach, *Briefe und Telegramme Wilhelms II an Nikolaus II—1898-1914;* Pokrovsky, *Perepiska Vilgelma vtorogo s Nikolaem vtorym.*

had been placed on Russian soil; but the tsar realized that at almost any moment the Japanese could attack Sakhalin. It was important, he felt, that the meeting occur as soon as possible.[42]

Roosevelt was overjoyed at Meyer's subsequent cable and informed the Russian ambassador, who only a few days before had said that Russia was not interested. Cassini insisted that Meyer had misquoted the tsar, but the president set aside Cassini's opinion. Lamsdorff confirmed the tsar's decision.[43] The president set up machinery for negotiation and held an audience with Takahira who said the Japanese gladly would name representatives to a conference. The president thought he had neared the end of his enterprise and sent identic notes to Russia and Japan on June 8. "The President feels that the time has come when in the interest of all mankind he must endeavor to see if it is not possible to bring an end to the terrible and lamentable conflict now being waged." He urged the Russian and Japanese governments, not only for their own sakes but in the interest of the civilized world, to negotiate directly. Within days both countries agreed to appoint representatives.[44] There were to be direct negotiations, place to be decided. Roosevelt was not accepted as mediator, nor had he any intention of serving as one.

Aside from help by the kaiser, Speck von Sternburg, and Meyer, it was a personal victory for Roosevelt.[45] Meyer noted in his diary a victory for the president.[46]

[42] Meyer to TR, June 9, 1905, TR MSS.

[43] TR to Lodge, June 16, 1905, Lodge MSS; and Lamsdorff to Cassini, June 10, 1905 (#8), *Sbornik diplomaticheskikh dokumentov.*

[44] Loomis to Meyer, and Griscom, June 8, 1905, SDA NA; Komura to Takahira, June 10, 1905 (#10857), Telegram Series, Reels for 1905, Japanese Foreign Ministry Archives; Griscom to TR, June 10, 1905, SDA NA; and Meyer to TR, June 12, 1905, TR MSS.

[45] TR to Charlemagne Tower, June 24, 1905, TR MSS.

[46] Meyer Diary, June 10, 1905, Meyer MSS LC.

The press and diplomats, Meyer continued, had been skeptical. The British had done little. Lansdowne who was unaware that the Japanese had prompted the mediation thought the attempts by Roosevelt to bring peace were ill-advised and had given no encouragement to Lodge, in Europe on vacation but charged by the president to persuade the British to recommend peace to the Japanese.[47] Later Lansdowne was saying that it was impossible to form any opinion until the effect of the catastrophe to the fleet was known.[48] As for the French, they were busy with internal politics—Delcassé left office on June 6. With announcement of the agreement to negotiate, even the British praised Roosevelt. "Mr. Roosevelt's success has amazed everybody," the London *Morning Post* noted. "He has displayed . . . great tact, great foresight, and finesse really extraordinary. Alone—absolutely without assistance or advice—he met every situation as it arose, shaped events to suit his purpose, and showed remarkable patience, caution, and moderation. As a diplomatist Mr. Roosevelt is now entitled to take high rank."[49]

47 Lodge Diary, March 29, 1905, Lodge MSS; and TR to Lodge, June 5 and 16, and July 11, 1905, Lodge MSS.

48 Lansdowne to Durand, June 5, 1905 (#75), *British Documents on the Origins of the War, 1898-1914*, IV.

49 London *Morning Post,* June 12, 1905, TR Scrapbooks, TR MSS.

Chapter Four

DETAILS

Whistle softly. We are getting into the thin timber, but we are not yet out of the woods.[1]

IF WITH AGREEMENT for a parley, the president and belligerents still had to work out details, Roosevelt's satisfaction led him to write his son Kermit that "with infinite labor and by the exercise of a good deal of tact and judgment—if I do say it myself—I have finally gotten the Japanese and Russians to agree to meet to discuss the terms of peace."[2] But as frequently happens in diplomacy, both sides tried to regain prestige: the Russians and Japanese dragged their feet over matters of minor importance. Roosevelt told Spring Rice that the experience was worse than getting a treaty passed by the United States Senate.[3]

The principal detail of the conference was its location, and such a controversy arose over this single matter that it threatened to postpone the meeting. The Russians wanted to meet in Europe, the Japanese in Asia. Another detail was the time of meeting. Another, how to choose delegates and determine their powers. Another, the question of an armistice. In all these matters, as in the rest of the negotiation, Roosevelt's was the dominant influence. He resembled a circus juggler as he solved these problems. It is remarkable, of course, that he rarely let his diplomatic efforts interfere with his own responsibilities as president, for he continued his regular duties in Washington.

IN DISCUSSION with Kaneko the president saw that European capitals—Paris, Berlin, and London—would be unacceptable sites for the negotiation. Mukden (Japanese-held) and Harbin (Russian-held) were not possible because of their proximity to the battlefields, the scene of Japanese victories. Kaneko had suggested Chefoo in North China, but said that Washington would be acceptable.[4] The Russians preferred Europe, particularly the capital of their ally, Paris. Roosevelt suggested The Hague, far better than any other place, he thought, because it was closely associated with the international arbitration tribunal and in a small neutral state. In Washington each side would expect Roosevelt to do the impossible, whereas at The Hague he perhaps could render assistance at some critical moment. The Japanese were intent on keeping the meeting out of Europe and again noted their preference for the United States, halfway between Europe and Asia. Roosevelt told Takahira that if he were in their place he would have accepted The Hague, or for that matter Paris, being only too glad to give the Russians the shell as long as he kept the kernel.[5]

Then the Russians asked for Washington. Cassini handed the president a cable on June 13 indicating that the place was of secondary importance because plenipotentiaries were to negotiate directly. "If Paris, so desirable for many reasons, encounters opposition, then the Imperial Government gives the preference to Washington over all other cities, especially since the presence of the President, initiator of the meeting, can exercise a bene-

1 New York *Times*, Aug. 31, 1905.

2 TR to Kermit Roosevelt, June 11, 1905, TR MSS.

3 TR to Spring Rice, June 16, 1905, TR MSS.

4 Kaneko interview with TR, June 7, 1905, "Kaneko Dan to Bei Daitōryō to no kaiken shimatsu," Kaneko Reel MT804, Japanese Foreign Ministry Archives.

5 TR to Kermit Roosevelt, June 14, 1905, and Kaneko to TR, June 14, 1905, TR MSS; and TR to Lodge, June 16, 1905, Lodge MSS.

ficial influence toward the end which we all have in view."[6]

This did not end the controversy. The city of Washington had its drawbacks, such as the well-known American liking for the Japanese and the more-than-beneficial influence that Roosevelt might exercise on a Washington conference. An Associated Press dispatch from St. Petersburg reported the question of the meeting place had been reopened and there was a possibility of The Hague. Exchanges, it said mysteriously, were proceeding.[7] Ambassador Meyer met Lamsdorff, unaware that the Russians had suggested Washington and that both Roosevelt and the Japanese had accepted. Meyer said the president was doing all he could to get The Hague. Lamsdorff said the Russians preferred The Hague because of the distance, because Washington was unbearable on account of the summer heat, and because they also were changing ambassadors (Baron Roman Rosen was to replace Cassini).[8] Roosevelt at this time wrote a friend that he had hard sledding getting the governments together, and that he was exasperated by such an antic. He had explained the folly of haggling to both the Russians and the Japanese. In another letter he exploded to Henry Cabot Lodge that Russia was so incompetent that he was unable to say if there would be peace.[9]

Meyer, who was now aware of the initial Russian acceptance of Washington, and Lamsdorff had an exchange in the solemn offices of the Foreign Ministry, where the foreign minister implied that Cassini had gone beyond his instructions. Lamsdorff agreed to send Meyer's note

[6] Lamsdorff to Cassini, June 13, 1905 (#12), *Sbornik diplomaticheskikh dokumentov;* and Cassini to TR, June 15, 1905, TR MSS.

[7] A.P. dispatch in TR to Lodge, June 16, 1905, Lodge MSS; see also New York *Times,* June 18, 1905.

[8] Meyer to TR, June 16 and 18, 1905, TR MSS.

[9] TR to Benjamin Wheeler, June 17, 1905, TR MSS; and TR to Lodge, June 16, 1905, Lodge MSS.

—terming as extraordinary the Russian action trying to make the president reverse his decision—to the tsar that afternoon.[10] At midnight Meyer heard Nicholas's answer. "I am pleased to inform your excellency," the note said, "that His Majesty the Emperor has no opposition to the choice of Washington for the meeting and discussions of the Plenipotentiaries of Russia and Japan." Lamsdorff said that he had just telegraphed the same to Cassini. Next day the Russian ambassador turned up at the White House with a note expressing the same ideas, but spoke of rumors in the press, as if his government had not informed Roosevelt it desired to change to The Hague.[11] "What I cannot understand about the Russian," Roosevelt lamented, "is the way he will lie when he knows perfectly well that you know he is lying."[12]

The location problem rattled on. The conference apparently could be held in the United States. But where? Roosevelt worried about the summer heat. To Cassini he wrote about some northern locality. The Portsmouth (N.H.) *Herald* reported a search for a location on the seashore.[13] Many cities were interested, and Bar Harbor and Portland offered their attractions. Mayor F. P. Story of Atlantic City proposed all courtesies to the peace commission.[14] Roosevelt wrote Takahira that he was taking steps to try to choose some cool, comfortable, retired

10 TR to Meyer, June 16, 1905, Meyer MSS and (#19), *Sbornik diplomaticheskikh dokumentov;* and Meyer to TR, June 18, 1905, TR MSS.

11 Lamsdorff to Meyer, June 17, 1905; the original of this letter is in the back flap of Meyer's Diary in Meyer MSS LC; it appears as (#23), *Sbornik diplomaticheskikh dokumentov;* see also Lamsdorff to Cassini, June 17, 1905 (#22), *Sbornik diplomaticheskikh dokumentov;* Meyer to TR, June 18, 1905, and Cassini to TR, June 17, 1905, TR MSS; and TR to Lodge, June 16, 1905, Lodge MSS—this letter to Lodge was actually written later, for it contains events up to June 18.

12 TR to Lodge, June 16, 1905, Lodge MSS.

13 TR to Cassini, June 15, 1905, TR MSS; and Portsmouth *Herald,* July 7, 1905.

14 New York *Times,* June 18, 1905; and Senator John T. Dryden to TR, in Hay to Loeb, June 22, 1905, TR MSS.

place for the meeting, where conditions would be agreeable and there would be as little interruption as possible.[15] Some of the better known resorts might make negotiation a spectacle. The Portsmouth *Herald* noted the distractions of Newport and Bar Harbor: "the men who are to consider terms of peace between the two great powers desire seclusion. Solitude is not necessary, but resorts like Newport are far too crowded and noisy for the deliberations of the embassy."[16] Later there was mention that Roosevelt feared that the smart set in the resorts would fete the Russian delegates because they were white, and neglect the Japanese.[17]

The need for communication facilities tended to limit sites to federal property, such as a navy yard; one town that fulfilled these requirements was Portsmouth, New Hampshire. Charged by the president to examine possible locations, Assistant Secretary of State Herbert H. D. Peirce checked with Western Union about increasing wire facilities to Portsmouth. He examined the town, and asked the New Hampshire secretary of state, Edward N. Pearson, to sound out the people of the area.[18] The Portsmouth *Herald* on July 7, 1905, made the first specific mention of the city as a location of the conference.

PEACE ENVOYS' MEETING
IS LIKELY TO BE HELD AT HOTEL WENTWORTH, NEW CASTLE
RUSSIAN AND JAPANESE ENVOYS TO CONFER IN THIS LOCALITY
WASHINGTON DISPATCH TO THE HERALD ASKS FOR LOCAL
INFORMATION

15 TR to Takahira, June 15, 1905, TR MSS.

16 Portsmouth *Herald*, July 8, 1905.

17 Sergei Witte, *Vospominaniia* [Memoirs], 3 vols. (Moscow, 1960), II, 423; see also the New York *Times*, July 7, 1905. Surprisingly this point was not discussed at all in the president's correspondence, though certainly the president must have been aware of the possibility.

18 R. C. Clowry (president of the Western Union in New York) to H. F. Taff (manager in Washington), June 30, 1905, and Edward Pearson to Herbert Peirce, July 3, 1905, TR MSS.

THE ISLES OF SHOALS ALSO A POSSIBLE SELECTION—
CONFERENCE TO BE HELD ABOUT AUGUST 1

The *Herald* announced on July 10 that the Russian and Japanese delegates would gather in Portsmouth for the greatest international meeting of the century. The scene would be the new equipment store building at the navy yard, where a marine guard would protect the envoys from interruption and the meetings would be secret. The paper noted the navy yard's telephone, telegraph, and wireless, and even the transatlantic cable station at Rye Beach—every possible means of communication.[19]

On Wednesday, July 12, 1905, Assistant Secretary Peirce announced the choice of Portsmouth, sessions to be held in the new building of the navy yard. The *Herald* dryly commented that Peirce had made one error: he should have known that the government had no navy yard in Portsmouth, N.H. It had one in Kittery, Maine, in the neighborhood of Portsmouth. The government at Washington was powerful, the paper admitted, but it could not take part of one state and annex it to another.[20] Governor John McLane formally invited the delegates to convene in the state of New Hampshire.[21]

Portsmouth, located on a flat plain in the southern part of New Hampshire, bordered the Atlantic; here was the Piscataqua river valley, the meeting of the waters from the Newichwannock, Bellamy, Oyster, Lamprey, and Squamscot rivers, which flowed into the Great Bay and the Atlantic. A citizen of the area suggested to the Portsmouth *Daily Chronicle* that a treaty between the Russians and Japanese should be known as "the Treaty of Piscataqua."[22] It was, and still is, a beautiful and quiet city.

19 Portsmouth *Herald,* July 7, 1905, as well as July 10 and 11, 1905.
20 Portsmouth *Herald,* July 12, 1905.
21 Portsmouth *Daily Chronicle,* July 13, 1905.
22 Thomas C. Wilson, *The Peace of Portsmouth* (Portsmouth, 1957), 4.

Buildings were old New England—gay-colored frame houses. The better houses were in the center of the town, in contrast to cities of today. Streets were winding and shaded by trees. The air was moist and fresh, and nearness to the water encouraged fishing—evident on the menus of local restaurants. Portsmouth's shores were low, rocky, and would remind a member of the Russian delegation (I. I. Korostovetz, secretary to the Russian first plenipotentiary) of the Finnish coast.[23] It was a model town, the best of life in country and city. It had the peace, beauty, and friendliness of a country village and at the same time the shopping, transport, and amusements of a metropolis.

The navy yard in Kittery, a small town founded in the seventeenth century, across the bay, years later would receive unwanted publicity for having reconditioned the atomic submarine *Thresher,* just before it sank into deep water in the Atlantic with the loss of the entire crew. In the old days the yard had a better reputation. For many years its docks and machine shops were the largest single industry north of Boston. The yard had opened in 1800 and twelve years later launched its first vessel, the *Washington.* With the decline of the navy in the years before the Civil War its importance lessened, but the Civil War brought life to the area: twenty-six vessels were the yard's contribution to the war, and one of them was the *Kearsarge* which defeated the *Alabama* off Cherbourg in 1864. Years later the Spanish-American War again momentarily brought the yard to life.

The scene of negotiation, the peace building, now houses submarine design offices and is known simply as building #86—the Shipyard Administration Building.

[23] *Korostovetz Diary,* Aug. 8, 1905: full title—I. I. Korostovetz, *Pre-war Diplomacy; the Russo-Japanese Problem; Treaty Signed at Portsmouth, U.S.A.* (London, 1920).

Part of the Japanese Delegation

(Standing, left to right: *Commander Ksaniu Takashita, Naval attaché; Henry Willard Denison, an American employed as legal adviser by the Japanese Foreign Office; Kotaro Konishi, attaché of the Japanese Legation;* Seated, left to right: *Takahira, Komura)*

COURTESY OF THE PISCATAQUA HISTORICAL SOCIETY

The Russian Diplomatic Staff

(Seated, left to right: *Witte, Rosen*)

COURTESY OF THE PISCATAQUA HISTORICAL SOCIETY

Meeting of the Delegates, August 14, 1905

COURTESY OF THE MCDONOUGH COLLECTION,
PISCATAQUA HISTORICAL CLUB

The Peace Building

COURTESY OF THE PISCATAQUA HISTORICAL CLUB

In 1905 it was a fine new brick structure, even though overhanging telephone wires and railroad tracks in front marred its beauty. The rooms for negotiation were simple but comfortable, heavy and dark drapes over the windows, long tables and leather-covered swivel chairs filled the rooms, electric fans hung down from wall brackets. Inelegant by present-day standards, this building in its heyday in 1905 led Korostovetz to comment that "one cannot help admiring the contrast of the American surroundings and ours especially as compared to the poor premises of the Russian Foreign Office."[24]

Delegates would stay at the Hotel Wentworth in New Castle, about two and a half miles from Portsmouth. Still in business at the present time, and well worth a trip to Portsmouth, it was, at the turn of the century, one of the finest resort hotels in the United States, easily as impressive as other spas American-style, such as the Broadmoor in Colorado Springs or French Lick in Southern Indiana. The Wentworth had opened in 1867. Guest lists read like a *Who's Who* of eastern society. On a hill overlooking the bay stood the huge white frame structure of four stories divided into three sections joined by roofed-in passages. It filled to capacity—it had accommodations for 400—during the summer months. It had attractive grounds; golf links, a swimming pool, fishing and boating on the sound.[25] Marring the beauty of the building in 1905 was the mosquito netting over each window, a symbol of the only drawback of the area. Ballrooms, where a large orchestra played, and dining areas were in elegant nineteenth-century Victorian style. The rooms had low ceilings and were simply furnished. With difficulty did the management in 1905 persuade some season guests to give up their places in favor of the peace delegation.

24 *Ibid.*
25 New York *Times,* May 6, 1905.

Portsmouth's main hotel, the Rockingham, a red-brick structure, housed most of the reporters covering the conference. The Rockingham is today much as in 1905—huge carpet-covered staircases, high ceilings, large baths, a fine old oak of a hostelry.

The time of the conference was quickly agreed upon. The Japanese wanted the conference to be held as soon as possible, and Komura told Griscom the plenipotentiaries would reach Washington in the first ten days of August. He asked if the president could get the Russian delegates there, and Hay cabled Meyer asking whether the Russian government agreed. Meyer communicated the same to Count Lamsdorff, and Nicholas found this date too distant. Roosevelt asked the Japanese to have their envoys present on the first day of August.[26]

The next detail was the delegates' powers. The Japanese feared that the Russian delegates might have only limited powers. Roosevelt told Cassini that the Japanese had sent full power to negotiate peace subject to ratification, hoping the Russians would give a similar power. Cassini for once was ready; in addition to handing Roosevelt a note indicating that the tsar would name representatives of high rank, he reminded Roosevelt that the word *plenipotentiary* meant that the Russian delegates would have full power.[27] The Japanese government was still not convinced about Russian intentions, as appears in a memorandum of Roosevelt to Meyer dated June 23 in which the president noted that Japanese plenipotentiaries would be of highest rank, and told Meyer to inform

[26] Griscom to State Department, June 18, 1905, SDA NA; Hay to Meyer, June 24, 1905, Meyer MSS; Meyer to Lamsdorff, June 25, 1905 (#37), and Lamsdorff to Meyer, June 25, 1905 (#39), *Sbornik diplomaticheskikh dokumentov;* Meyer to TR, June 25, 1905, TR MSS; and TR to Meyer, June 26, 1905, Meyer MSS.

[27] Takahira to TR, June 14, 1905, TR to Cassini, June 15, 1905, and TR to Takahira, June 15, 1905, TR MSS.

the Russian Foreign Office that the wording of the Russian announcement evidently made the Japanese doubt whether the Russian plenipotentiaries would have equal power.[28]

The belligerents meanwhile had to choose their plenipotentiaries. Prime Minister Taro Katsura had hoped to name Ito who then was chairman of the Privy Council, with Foreign Minister Komura as his colleague. Ito was Japan's most famous statesman. The Russians were familiar with his efforts for closer Russo-Japanese relations. The St. Petersburg correspondent of the London *Daily Telegraph,* E. J. Dillon, acting on behalf of Count Witte, approached Minister Hayashi in London to ask Ito's appointment. Roosevelt hoped Ito would be the Japanese representative.[29] Ito declined, feeling that Katsura should retain responsibility for the war as Ito had done in the Sino-Japanese War of 1894-1895, especially since before the war Ito had been unsympathetic with Katsura's Russian policy.[30] Ito and Katsura had the same object—forcing the Russians to make some settlement in Manchuria and Korea—but differed on the means. Ito had recommended an alliance with the Russians instead of the British. He thought any diplomatic approach to Britain might lead to war with Russia and offered little in return, for the British had no real interest in Korea. Even if the Japanese pursued such a connection Ito felt there could be an additional alliance with St. Petersburg. He worked for this goal in the prewar period and visited the Russian capital in 1901. The difficulties were never overcome, and even Ito came to view the Far Eastern war

28 TR to Meyer, June 23 and 26, 1905, Meyer MSS.

29 E. J. Dillon, *The Eclipse of Russia* (New York, 1918), 301; and TR to Meyer, July 18, 1905, Meyer MSS.

30 Tokyo *Asahi,* June 16, 1905, also June 19 and 25, 1905, as cited in Tatsuji Takeuchi, *War and Diplomacy in the Japanese Empire* (New York, 1935), 151.

as necessary. Still he preached rapprochement, and throughout the war called for peace—he made several attempts to end the war.

Katsura then named Komura chief plenipotentiary. The background of the chief Japanese delegate was interesting. His father, the owner of a sawmill in Kyushu, had intended that the son inherit and manage the mill, but the lord of the Obi clan to which the family belonged sent young Komura to Nanko Daigaku, the predecessor of Tokyo University. From there Komura went to the Harvard Law School and graduated in 1878. After a brief service as a judge he entered the Foreign Office where he was to spend the rest of his public life. His posts included Washington, St. Petersburg, Peking, and Seoul. Small and frail, he had mannerisms that led Dillon to observe "the opaqueness of the professional diplomat,"[31] but he was a man of action, impatient with delay, with remarkable force of mind and ability to see the essence of a problem. His long diplomatic experience also had taught him to compromise.

Reaction to Komura's appointment was favorable. Roosevelt wrote Meyer that appointment of Komura represented the highest appointment the Japanese government could make, equivalent to his appointing the secretary of state.[32] Komura was well equipped to negotiate Japan's demands at the forthcoming peace conference. As coarchitect, with Katsura, of the nation's foreign policy, he knew why the Japanese had gone to war and what the Japanese wanted in the peace.

Katsura chose another Harvard graduate, the minister in Washington, Takahira, as second plenipotentiary. The

[31] Shoji Komura, "Jutaro Komura, My Father," *Contemporary Japan*, I (1933), 641-49; and E. J. Dillon, "Sergius Witte and Jutaro Komura," *Harper's Weekly*, XLIX (1905), 1262.

[32] TR to Meyer, June 26, 1905, Meyer MSS.

remaining members of the delegation indicated the sincere spirit in which the Japanese government entered the peace negotiations.[33] The delegation included Henry W. Denison, an American legal adviser to the Japanese Foreign Office and an expert on the Far East, who, the Portsmouth *Daily Chronicle* reported, was highly prized by the Japanese government. A native of Vermont, Denison had served in the consulate in Yokohama, and then in 1880 joined the Japanese Foreign Office where he held a post until his death in 1914. He had been honored for his work in the Sino-Japanese War and his part in negotiating the Anglo-Japanese Alliance of 1902. Other members of the delegation were Aimaro Sato, minister resident; Yenjiro Yamaza, director of the political bureau of the Foreign Office; Mineichiro Adachi, first secretary of the legation and counselor in the Foreign Office; Masanao Hanihara, third secretary of the legation; Colonel Koichiro Tachibana, connected with the war office; Kumataro Honda, secretary in the Foreign Office and private secretary to the minister of foreign affairs; and Kotaro Konishi, attaché of the legation. Katsura instructed Baron Kentaro Kaneko to continue his good publicity work with the American president.[34]

The Russians did not choose their delegates as easily, for the war had been so disastrous that many people thought the only acceptable settlement was victory. In the government there was no general desire for peace; court clique, grand dukes, the war party, and most of the tsar's ministers opposed peace, confident that General N. P. Linievich's reorganized Manchurian army could beat the Japanese. Only with difficulty were Witte and

33 Griscom to State Department, July 7, 1905, SDA NA.

34 Portsmouth *Daily Chronicle,* July 26, 1905; and Takahira to Katsura, July 4, 1905 (#12217), and Katsura to Takahira, July 3, 1905 (#12693), Telegram Series, Reels for 1905, Japanese Foreign Ministry Archives.

the peace party able to convince the tsar to proceed with the negotiations. To get someone to serve on the peace delegation was difficult. For the chief plenipotentiary the most obvious choice was Witte, but his position was similar to that of Ito. The war had been carried on under other leadership. Witte and the tsar were not intimate, and the tsar so disliked Witte that he would have preferred almost anyone else. When Lamsdorff recommended Witte as a possible first choice the tsar noted on the report: "not Witte."[35]

Lamsdorff's next suggestion was the ambassador to Paris, A. I. Nelidov, the oldest and highest in rank of all ambassadors, a man of much diplomatic experience. Meyer thought the appointment unfortunate: he had known Nelidov in Rome and considered him old and nervous. Nelidov had made a mess in Rome of the tsar's failure to return the visit of the king, handling it in such a way that it gave umbrage to the Italian people, and the king of Italy sent word that Nelidov was no longer persona grata.[36] His appointment to Portsmouth did go through, but Nelidov shortly resigned it on account of bad health, inability to speak English, and lack of knowledge of Far Eastern affairs.[37]

Lamsdorff then recommended the current Russian ambassador in Rome, N. V. Muraviev, nephew of the famous governor-general of Eastern Siberia under whose leadership Russia had acquired the Amur and Maritime regions. A former minister of justice, Muraviev returned to St. Petersburg to discuss the appointment. Meyer's reaction was favorable: "the appointment of Muravieff I hope will turn out to be a good one. The German Ambassador,"

[35] Foreign Ministry Memo, June 24, 1905 (#31), *Sbornik diplomaticheskikh dokumentov.*

[36] Meyer to TR, June 18, 1905, TR MSS.

[37] A. I. Nelidov to Lamsdorff, June 18 (#35) and June 26, 1905 (#40), *Sbornik diplomaticheskikh dokumentov.*

he continued, "told me before it was decided that he considered him to be the best man that they had in the diplomatic service. He is also spoken of as the future Minister of Foreign Affairs to succeed Lamsdorff."[38] Still, Muraviev decided to decline because, he said, he felt poorly qualified. Significantly he told Minister of Finance V. N. Kokovtsov that the 15,000 rouble allowance was inadequate.[39]

The search continued, and by this time resembled a search for a scapegoat. Lamsdorff considered Alexander Iswolsky, but the future foreign minister hastily made known his intent to refuse. Witte suggested Lamsdorff's assistant, Prince Obolensky, and D. D. Pokotilov, the Russian minister in Peking.[40] Neither was willing.

As possible candidates disappeared the emperor found himself forced to turn to Witte, who commented to Kokovtsov that "when a sewer has to be cleaned, they send Witte; but as soon as work of a cleaner and nicer kind appears, plenty of other candidates spring up."[41] Sergei Iulievich Witte was a descendant of a Dutch family in the Baltic provinces. His father was a government official, the manager of a model state farm in Saratov province, who had acquired hereditary nobility. Witte had attended Novorossiisk University, and in 1871 entered government service with the rank of titular counselor. This service lasted only until 1877 when he took up railroad work. He went back to the government in 1889 to take charge of Russian railways, was minister of finance from 1892 to 1902, and became the architect of Russia's new industry. In appearance he was a contrast to the

[38] Meyer to TR, July 1, 1905, TR MSS.

[39] Lamsdorff to Roman Rosen, July 12, 1905 (#64), *Sbornik diplomaticheskikh dokumentov;* and V. N. Kokovtsov, *Out of My Past* (Stanford, 1935), 52-53.

[40] Witte, *Vospominaniia,* II, 393-95.

[41] Kokovtsov, *Out of My Past,* 52-53.

chief Japanese delegate, Komura. Witte was a huge robust man of about six feet six, manner gruff and blunt after years of domination in economic and political affairs. He treated others as juniors and inferiors. The diminutive, reserved Komura appeared no match for him.

Reaction to Witte's appointment, as with that of Komura, was favorable. Witte impressed Meyer; Roosevelt told Meyer he was glad Witte was coming.[42] Witte, of course, had long been connected with Russia's Far Eastern interests and had much knowledge of the area. In fact Witte had been largely responsible for establishing the Russian sphere of interest in that part of the world, before the war with the Japanese. As minister of finance he worked for Russian commercial dominance in Asia. But Witte had fallen from power and more ambitious elements took over Russian Far Eastern policy and brought on the war. Witte had counseled compromise with the Japanese but the tsar followed other advice. Witte then had preached peace throughout the war. Despite his disagreements with the Russian government he was still well prepared to negotiate a treaty for the Far East.

Witte would have a good staff. His chief assistant, the second Russian plenipotentiary, was the new ambassador in Washington, Baron Rosen, whose selection was first announced at the time of Nelidov's acceptance. He had been consul general in New York City and chargé in Washington, and had served as minister to Mexico, Greece, Serbia, Rumania, and Japan, where he was when the war broke out. Meyer predicted that Rosen, a Baltic German by background, would be much liked and was a great improvement over Cassini. "I understand Japan thinks well of him and he has a great respect for them."[43]

[42] Meyer Diary, July 16, 1905, Meyer MSS LC; and TR to Meyer, July 18, 1905, Meyer MSS.

[43] Meyer Diary, June 9, 1905, Meyer MSS LC; and Meyer to TR, June 18, 1905, TR MSS.

Other members of the delegation were F. F. de Martens, the well-known professor of international law at St. Petersburg University as well as privy counselor and member of the council of foreign ministry; I. P. Shipov, privy counselor and chief of the treasury division of the ministry of finance; Pokotilov, minister in Peking; G. A. Planson, former head of the diplomatic chancellery of Viceroy Evgenii Alekseiev and consul general in Korea; I. I. Korostovetz, formerly secretary of the legation in Peking and a veteran of trips to America in 1894 and 1901; and the military advisers A. I. Rusin and M. K. Samoilov.[44]

Roosevelt had made no mention of halting hostilities, and Lamsdorff in June asked Meyer about this problem. The foreign minister's idea was for belligerent armies to be tranquil, with a neutral zone between them. Each would keep the right to send up troops, ammunition, and supplies. Lamsdorff wanted the president's opinion as to procedure, because the Russians and Japanese were not in communication.[45] But the Japanese suspected a Russian intention to improve the military forces in Manchuria. The president notified Meyer he had done his best to get Japanese assent and that the Japanese were confident they could win what they wished, whereas they deeply distrusted the Russian sincerity. Russia at all costs had to make peace. The tsar had to turn his attention from the war to internal affairs. If he did not, Roosevelt wrote, the disaster to Russia would make the country cease to count among the great powers for a generation. To Spring Rice he wrote, "I made an honest effort to get them an armistice, but I am forced to say that from Japan's standpoint I think that Japan was absolutely right in refusing it. . . . It may be that there will have to be one more crushing defeat of the Russian army in Manchuria be-

[44] Portsmouth *Herald*, July 17, 1905.
[45] TR to Meyer, June 23, 1905, Meyer MSS.

fore the Russians wake up to the fact that peace is a necessity."[46] At Japanese insistence there would be no armistice until shortly before the signature of the peace treaty, something of an unusual procedure.

[46] TR to Meyer, July 7, 1905, Meyer MSS; and TR to Spring Rice, July 24, 1905, TR MSS.

Chapter Five

ROOSEVELT AND THE JAPANESE

As for Japan, she has risen with simply marvelous rapidity, and she is as formidable from the industrial as from the military standpoint. She is a great civilized nation; though her civilization is in some important respects not like ours.[1]

IT WAS STRANGE to observe a president of the United States trying to flatter and cajole the Japanese, seeking to give them the feeling of being a great nation and, at the same time, to make them as susceptible to suggestion as if they were one of the little powers of Latin America. Such was Theodore Roosevelt's task in the summer of 1905. It was a long way, in history and in diplomacy, from the bluff and hearty years of the mid-nineteenth century when Commodore Matthew C. Perry was making speeches before and after going to Japan, telling what he was going to do or had done on his voyage of opening up that part of the world. Time was when a few gunboats, the famed ships with their black, sooty smoke, belching out their tidings of civilization to the unappreciative Japanese, could strike terror into the subjects of the mikado. Now the Emperor Meiji was an old man surrounded by wise old men who had helped take Japan from feudalism to modern ways, and these latter individuals were talking to President Roosevelt as equals, and *mirabile dictu* the president was talking to them as if they were equals.

During the summer months of 1905 Roosevelt, who had been born four years after Perry's treaty with the

Japanese, was seeking to convince the Island Empire of the need of peace. He was urging the Japanese to be kind to the Russians, to be moderate in the terms presented to Count Witte at the forthcoming Portsmouth Conference. This made for an interesting summer.

After the battle of Tsushima there was much American apprehension about the continuance of the war. The president worried that the Russians, if they refused peace, would lose all their Far Eastern possessions, leaving the Japanese dominant in East Asia and a threat to American possessions. He hoped that the Japanese terms would not force the tsar to continue the war.[2] The president held discussions with Kaneko about moderating the Japanese demands.[3] Kaneko's assurances did not satisfy Roosevelt, and after telling his son Kermit of the difficulty of getting the belligerents to negotiate he expressed his fear that the Japanese would ask too much.[4] He wrote Spring Rice he thought that Tsushima would be a fight rather than a slaughter. The Japanese were well prepared: "In a dozen years the English, Americans and Germans, who now dread one another as rivals in the trade of the Pacific, will have each to dread the Japanese more than they do any other nation." He marveled that the Japanese in the middle of the war had increased their exports to China and established new lines of steamers which were not allowed to compete with one another. Japanese industrial growth, he believed, was as great as its military growth. While the Japanese would act with motives and ways of thought not quite like those of the white powers, he hoped that Japan would take its place as a great power.

[1] TR to Lodge, June 16, 1905, Lodge MSS.

[2] TR to Meyer, June 19, 1905, Meyer MSS.

[3] Kaneko interviews with TR, June 7 and July 7, 1905, "Kaneko Dan to Bei Daitōryō to no kaiken shimatsu," Kaneko Reel MT804, Japanese Foreign Ministry Archives.

[4] TR to Kermit Roosevelt, June 11, 1905, TR MSS.

He wanted Americans to treat the Japanese with courtesy, generosity, and justice. He intended to keep a strong navy and wanted every ship at highest possible efficiency as a fighting unit. To bluster, he wrote, to treat the Japanese as an inferior and alien race as did many Americans, while not keeping the military at high efficiency, would invite a disaster.[5] So far as concerned the war, he believed that if it lasted another year the Japanese would drive the Russians out of Eastern Asia but receive no indemnity. They would have the strain of an extra year's losses, and no usable territory. They would have the expense of defending this new territory, since the Russians would look for an opportunity to regain it.[6] Also Japan would have virtual control of East Asia and would threaten American interests.

Roosevelt was not aware how important an extra year's losses had become. He was not informed about internal conditions in Japan and did not realize the extent of the financial crisis. Foreign money had supplied more than half the military expenditures raised by loans. Early in the war the Japanese easily had raised loans. With the help of Jacob H. Schiff of Kuhn, Loeb, and Company, the vice governor of the Bank of Japan, Viscount Korekiyo Takahashi, raised 97 million yen at 6 percent interest in May of 1904 and 117 million yen under the same terms in November. In March 1905, at the time of the battle of Mukden, the Japanese floated a loan: 292 million yen at 4½ percent interest. Katsura concluded another loan in July 1905, 292 million yen at 4½ percent interest. But the national debt rose from 600 million yen to over 2 billion, with annual interest of about 110 million.[7] It

[5] TR to Spring Rice, June 16, 1905, TR MSS.

[6] TR to Reid, July 7, 1905, Reid MSS.

[7] Gataro Ogawa, *Expenditures of the Russo-Japanese War* (New York, 1923), 51-71.

was apparent in Tokyo, though not in Washington, that the war was too expensive. To be sure, this fear for the expense of the war occurred in that era's thin climate of financial knowledge. It later became evident—though not until the Second World War—that nations around the world, Germany and Japan and the United States, could raise larger sums internally than anyone dreamed in 1905. Neither the Japanese in 1905 nor anyone else knew how to manage an economy, and there was fear of national bankruptcy.

Outwardly the Japanese seemed at the peak of their military strength, but despite such successes Katsura and the cabinet wanted peace. In Manchuria the military planners knew after the battle of Mukden that they had reached the limit of their striking power. The army informed Tokyo in March 1905 that any new military move would require more forces.[8] The victory at Mukden was indecisive because the Japanese commander could not follow up. Russian forces were increasing rapidly, and the Japanese feared that the quality of Russian troops was improving. Planners estimated that crack Russian troops were in Europe because of revolutionary threats and fear of the Germans. At the beginning of the Russo-Japanese War the troops in the Far East were at best second-line. There was an improving situation on the Trans-Siberian. The tedious water-and-ice route across Lake Baikal was no more; in the autumn of 1904 the Russians completed a line around the lake.[9] Since the outbreak of war the Russian ministry of communication had built sidetracks which had the effect of doubletracking, solving the most difficult problem on the long line.

If for such reasons the Japanese government decided

[8] Gaimusho [Foreign Ministry], *Komura Gaikoshi* [A History of Komura's Diplomacy], 2 vols. (Tokyo, 1953), II, 114.

[9] *Ibid.*, 110-13.

on peace after Tsushima, this state of affairs was not apparent to the president. As June and July 1905 passed and peace seemed remote, Roosevelt told Meyer that the Japanese would take Vladivostok and Harbin if the war continued. The British, he thought, had encouraged the Japanese to ask for too much. Concerned over Lansdowne's refusal to press Tokyo, the president wrote Reid in London that it would be better for Britain to have peace, with the Russians face to face with the Japanese in East Siberia. Such a result combined with the Anglo-Japanese alliance would prevent any Russian move toward India or Persia. If the Japanese took Siberia they would have done all damage possible to Russia, and the Anglo-Japanese alliance would be worthless.[10] Roosevelt wrote to Spring Rice in St. Petersburg, "Don't you think you go a little needlessly into heroics when you say that 'claims of honor . . . commands England to abstain from putting any pressure whatever upon Japan to abstain from action which may eventually entail severe sacrifices on England's part?' " All he asked was pressure such as the Germans and French had put on the tsar. Roosevelt agreed with the British that it was necessary to prevent a hostile combination against the Japanese, and he had taken measures to stop such a combine. He failed to understand the difference in position which made it proper for France as the ally of Russia to urge the Russians to make peace, and yet improper for Great Britain as the ally of Japan to urge the Japanese to make peace.[11] Should the war continue, the Japanese could not get an indemnity large enough. Lansdowne's position was that Great Britain could take no attitude that would prove in remotest degree to the advantage of the Russians. However much

[10] TR to Meyer, June 19, 1905, Meyer MSS; and TR to Reid, July 7, 1905, Reid MSS.

[11] TR to Spring Rice, July 24, 1905, TR MSS.

the British wanted peace, for humanitarian or other reasons, loyalty to the Japanese prevented even pressure by suggestion. When the Japanese asked for advice the British prepared it, with Japan's interest the primary consideration.[12]

Not even the death of John Hay on July 1, 1905, after the secretary of state had returned from Europe and seemed on the way to recovery, could lessen Roosevelt's concern about the Japanese demands. By mid-July he again was telling Meyer he would try to get the Japanese to be moderate. The extreme war party in Japan insisted on driving the Russians off the Pacific slope. The moderates would accept what the Japanese had acquired in Manchuria and Korea plus Sakhalin and possibly an indemnity. Any terms, Roosevelt warned Meyer, would show a severe Russian defeat. He talked with Kaneko in early July about moderation and while conceding that a Japanese Monroe Doctrine should exclude the European powers from concessions, he warned against a Russian collapse.[13]

Newspapers reported that the Japanese minister in London, Hayashi, had intimated his country's readiness to continue the war.[14] By this time, late July, the peace conference was almost ready to meet. Writing to J. St. Loe

[12] Lansdowne to Spring Rice, Aug. 7, 1905, copy in TR MSS.

[13] TR to Meyer, July 18, 1905; see also TR to Meyer, June 19 and July 17, 1905, Meyer MSS; and Kaneko interview with TR, July 7, 1905, "Kaneko Dan to Bei Daitōryō to no kaiken shimatsu," Kaneko Reel MT804, Japanese Foreign Ministry Archives. Roosevelt tended to overemphasize the "war party" in Japan. Actually the Japanese military leaders were among the first to see the need for peace, since they had reached the limits of their striking power, and so advised Tokyo. Roosevelt never understood this. Indeed the civil government was more conservative than the military and echoed the call for peace only when convinced by the military. As Raymond Esthus has noted, "Japan's apparent intransigence in May, 1905, probably was caused more by a feeling of weakness than by intoxication over military victories." See Raymond A. Esthus, *Theodore Roosevelt and Japan* (Seattle, 1966), 66-70.

[14] Portsmouth *Herald,* July 19, 1905.

That Interview
as It Wasn't

Admiral Yamamoto: Good morning, Mr. President. We are going to have a war . . .
President Roosevelt: What's that?

Admiral Yamamoto: We are going to have a warm day today.
President Roosevelt: Oh, yes, yes! I think we are.

FROM A CARTOON HISTORY OF ROOSEVELT'S CAREER

President Roosevelt, The Peace Showman

"Here, ladies and gentlemen, is the newest attraction. This bear, a ravenous beast of prey subdued by Togo and Oyama, is now so tame that he subscribes to anything that is dictated to him."

FROM A CARTOON HISTORY OF ROOSEVELT'S CAREER

The Big Stick in a New Role

UNCLE SAM (looking at the olive branches wreathing the Roosevelt club): Well, I guess a little strenuosity is worthwhile in peace as well as in war.

FROM A CARTOON HISTORY OF ROOSEVELT'S CAREER

The End of the Peace Conference

FROM A CARTOON HISTORY OF ROOSEVELT'S CAREER

Strachey, the editor of the London *Spectator,* Roosevelt mentioned that the war was costing about two million yen a day and Japan could not possibly get an indemnity large enough to make an extension of the war worthwhile. If he controlled Japanese foreign policy he would decide whether he wanted eastern Siberia and otherwise he would introduce moderate demands. To the Russians anything else would be unacceptable. He had to convince the Tokyo government, he told Strachey, that an indemnity in comparison to Sakhalin, Port Arthur, and Dalny, overlordship of Korea, and succession to all Russian rights in Manchuria, amounted to little.[15]

The president spent June and July of 1905 in frustration. Unaware of conditions in Japan and the plans for Portsmouth, he could only advise and write letters to people he hoped would advise. It was at this time that he began to worry about the security of the Philippines and Hawaii, especially since the Japanese had displayed such capable naval power which could be turned against the Americans. Then there were the beginnings of the Japanese immigration crisis. Few Japanese immigrants were in the United States before 1898, but with the acquisition of Hawaii in that year the number had grown and by 1900 there were increasing protests. By 1904 nearly 8,000 Japanese were in the continental United States and the trouble became serious. The center of the protests was California, and in February 1905 the San Francisco *Chronicle* wrote about the subject; the next month it urged a limit to immigration. A resolution in the California state legislature called the immigrants "immoral, intemperate, quarrelsome men." It passed unanimously. The president was disgusted with the events in California and thought that state had acted "in the worst possible taste and in the most offensive manner

[15] TR to J. St. Loe Strachey, July 27, 1905, TR MSS.

to Japan." The president opposed discrimination in the United States and became concerned about the reaction of the Tokyo government. He wrote Griscom to tell the Japanese that the Washington government, and for that matter the American people, had "not the slightest sympathy with the outrageous agitation against the Japanese."[16]

Because of this fear that American security was in danger, the president asked Taft, then en route to Manila, to speak with Katsura. Griscom was unaware that Taft planned anything more than a courtesy call. Taft and party (over 75 people, including the president's daughter, 7 senators, and 24 congressmen) arrived in late July. Outwardly this was a social visit. The Japanese greeted the Americans enthusiastically, even wildly, as the delegation entered Tokyo. Flags waving and frequent banzais made a strong impression.[17] But it was more than a social visit, for a talk between Taft and Katsura dealt with Korea and changes relating to the war then in progress. Taft felt sure that Roosevelt would agree to a Japanese suzerainty over Korea. Katsura gave the strongest assurances that his government had no aspirations regarding the Philippines and Hawaii, and suggested that the United States join the Anglo-Japanese alliance, about to be renewed, in practice if not in name. Taft declared that such a course was difficult and indeed impossible because

[16] TR to Griscom, July 15, 1905, TR MSS; and Esthus, *Theodore Roosevelt and Japan,* 128-33. The Esthus book is the best account of the Japanese immigration crisis.

[17] Takahira to Komura, March 24, 1905 (#3100), Telegram Series, Reels for 1905, Japanese Foreign Ministry Archives; Lloyd Griscom, *Diplomatically Speaking* (Boston, 1940), 257-60; and Griscom to State Department, Aug. 5, 1905, SDA NA. For the best primary description of the trip, see Mabel Dubois to her mother, July 10 to Sept. 20, 1905—a diary type letter, William Howard Taft MSS in the Library of Congress. A good secondary description is R. E. Minger, "Taft's Missions to Japan: A Study in Personal Diplomacy," *Pacific Historical Review,* XXX (1961), 279-94.

of public opinion. The ensuing written agreement between the two men, which later became known as the Taft-Katsura Memorandum, repudiated the Korean-American treaty of 1882. It showed the president's sympathy for one of the Japanese war aims, the control of Korea. To Taft's cable informing the president of the substance of the meeting, Roosevelt answered: "absolutely correct in every respect. Wish you would state to Katsura that I confirm every word you have said."[18]

THE SUCCESS of the war led many Japanese to press their government in regard to the peace. Most of the political parties supported the war. Both houses of the Diet had passed resolutions of satisfaction with victories on land and sea, and appropriated a large war budget. The government strangely adopted a policy of declining to reply to parliamentary questions, and Katsura failed to deliver the traditional address on foreign relations at the November 1904 sitting of the Diet. Representative Kungoro Shigeoka declared in a budget committee meeting that the war was not private. Representative Yoshiro Kubota introduced a resolution, soon passed, to make public the diplomatic documents relating to the war. If the government failed to conduct foreign relations to the satisfaction of the public, he said, a violent conflict would lead to the government's fall.[19] Katsura refused; such a practice could only produce popular dissatisfaction and, even

[18] Taft to State Department, July 29, 1905, corrected first draft, and TR to Taft, July 31, 1905, Taft MSS; and Taro Katsura to Komura, Aug. 8, 1905 (#13026), Telegram Series, Reels for 1905, Japanese Foreign Ministry Archives. For the best secondary account, see Raymond A. Esthus, "The Taft-Katsura Agreement—Reality or Myth?," *Journal of Modern History*, XXXI (1959), 46-51.

[19] *Dai Nijuikkai Teikoku Gikai Shugiin Iinkaigiroku,* I, #1, 6, and *Teikoku Gikaishi,* VI, 205, 211-14, and 463, as cited in Tatsuji Takeuchi, *War and Diplomacy in the Japanese Empire* (New York, 1935), 147-48.

more important, impossible demands in the peace. This secretive policy eventually brought about the fall of Katsura, but after the Japanese signed the Portsmouth peace.

By the time of Tsushima the political parties and many other organizations had clear views concerning peace. People agreed on a large indemnity; Sakhalin and the Maritime provinces; Russian leases in Manchuria; Russian evacuation and renunciation of all rights in China. They expected the surrender of Russian vessels in neutral ports; a limit to any navy in the Pacific and Japan Sea; no cession or lease of Chinese territory without Japanese consent; no armistice before the signing of a peace treaty. Finally, the peace conference was to be in a place chosen by the Japanese. While the two major political parties, the *Seiyukai* and *Kensei Honto,* refused to declare themselves in detail, they issued enumerations of indemnity, cessions, and their proposed solutions of the Manchurian question. One group was more specific. Seven Tokyo University professors called for a harsh peace, including an indemnity of three billion yen; territory (including Sakhalin, Kamchatka, and the Maritime provinces in Siberia); the entire Russian Manchurian railroad; Russian commercial enterprises in Manchuria; restrictions of Russian army and navy forces east of Lake Baikal; and a prolongation of the war until peace was concluded. Many people expected the Japanese government to press for such demands. Organizations such as *Tairo Doshikai* passed resolutions to protest a dishonorable peace and called for hostilities until the imperial armies had subjugated the enemy.[20] Some Japanese, such as the Socialists, opposed the war. Socialism had emerged only after the war of 1894-1895. The small but boisterous

[20] Griscom to State Department, June 22 and 24, 1905, SDA NA; see also *Teikoku Gikaishi,* III, 443, and Tokyo *Asahi,* June 29, 1905, as cited in Takeuchi, *War and Diplomacy in the Japanese Empire,* 150.

group of Socialists subscribed to the ideal of universal peace. Newspapers such as *Heimin Shimbun* sought to convince the Japanese of the folly of war. They struggled against Katsura's government and asked immediate peace with no demands. They pointed to taxes and the human cost. Despite police harassment they continued until the government silenced *Heimin Shimbun* in late 1904, and several months later jailed some leaders including Danjiro Kōtoku.[21] The majority of Japanese not only supported the war but expected excessive gains from the peace.

The conditions the Japanese delegates presented Witte at Portsmouth were, of course, the result of private consideration. From the beginning Katsura and especially Komura thought of peace in an international perspective. They hoped for worldwide good will and wanted to ward off any third-power intervention.[22] As foreign minister in the unsuccessful attempts to avoid the war, Komura knew the difficulties of diplomacy. After the Japanese triumphs in the spring of 1904, he had worked out in consultation with Katsura a draft of objectives and peace demands. He assumed a victory, and his peace terms were more comprehensive than his war objectives. Approved by the cabinet in August, the terms included a demand for a sphere of influence in Manchuria—in contrast to prewar pledges of guarantee of the integrity of China. The Russians were to give up their lease on the Kwantung peninsula and the railroads between Port Arthur and Harbin and to withdraw from Manchuria. The Japanese were to have freedom in Korea.[23] By late August 1904 with the hopeful military outlook, another set of terms

[21] Hyman Kublin, "The Japanese Socialists and the Russo-Japanese War," *Journal of Modern History,* XXII (1950), 322-39.

[22] Hayashi to Komura, March 31, 1905 (#2810), Telegram Series, Reels for 1905, Japanese Foreign Ministry Archives: and Kaneko interview with TR, June 6, 1904, "Kaneko Dan to Bei Daitōryō to no kaiken shimatsu," Kaneko Reel MT804, Japanese Foreign Ministry Archives.

[23] Gaimusho, *Komura Gaikoshi,* II, 27.

called for a much larger position in Eastern Asia. The Russians were to have only commercial traffic on the Chinese Eastern Railway, preventing any military preparations, and were to recognize equality of commerce and industry for all nations and to return any occupied territory to China. The Japanese hoped to demand fishing rights in the Maritime provinces and navigation on the Amur River up to Blagoveshchensk. That town plus Khabarovsk and Nikolaevsk were to be free ports, and in these three localities as well as Vladivostok the Japanese could have consulates. Finally, the cession of Sakhalin and an indemnity.[24]

The Japanese government continually sounded the American government on peace terms, in an attempt to find out what the president would approve. Takahira in mid-January 1905 had talked about dominance in Korea, the open door in Manchuria, cession of Port Arthur. The president agreed that the Japanese had a right to hold Port Arthur. He did hope to see Manchuria restored to the Chinese and protected by the major powers. And the Kingdom of Korea, which in Roosevelt's mind had shown an inability to remain independent, was to come under Japanese control. Takahira talked further to Hay about peace terms. On Korea and Port Arthur there was an agreement. While the Japanese were reluctant to accept international control of Manchuria, the differences between Tokyo and Washington even on this item were slight.[25]

Roosevelt, wanting to make sure the Japanese understood his position, expressed his ideas to Richard Barry, a reporter for *Collier's,* with instructions that Barry should forward the president's views to the journalist George

[24] *Ibid.,* 27-28.

[25] TR to Meyer, Feb. 6, 1905, Meyer MSS; Meyer to Roosevelt, Jan. 20, 1905, TR MSS; Hay Diary, Jan. 26, 1905, Hay MSS.

Kennan (cousin of the present-day historian) in Tokyo who was to make Roosevelt's views known to "men of influence." Roosevelt was definite about Japanese retention of Port Arthur, and in reply to Barry's comment that the European powers might attempt to prevent the Japanese from keeping the city he said, "*I* would *make* her hold Port Arthur. She has won it, and it is hers, never to be surrendered again. . . . Japan must hold Port Arthur and she must hold Korea. These two points are already settled." Later Kennan wrote of a talk with Katsura, who restated Tokyo's intent not to ask exorbitant demands, only those that would guarantee the peaceful future. Katsura repeated that "His Majesty's Government must have some satisfactory assurance of safety and permanent peace."[26]

By March 1905 rumors were widespread about Japanese intentions to demand an indemnity. In an interview held shortly before the western trip, Roosevelt learned from Takahira that Tokyo would seek indemnity. The president was unenthusiastic and reserved his judgment. He warned that an indemnity demand might prolong the war, which in turn would use up more money. The Japanese persisted. Takahira talked about demands while Taft sat on the lid during the president's bear hunt. He said the Japanese would insist on an indemnity—history, he said, had no instance where the right of indemnity was clearer. Takahira mentioned Sakhalin.[27]

The Japanese sought advice from foreign groups which were representative of public opinion favoring the Tokyo government. One of their strongest supporters was the

[26] Richard Barry to Kennan, Feb. 21, 1905, George Kennan MSS in the Library of Congress; and George Kennan to TR, March 30, 1905, and Taft to TR, April 5, 1905, TR MSS.

[27] TR to Hay, April 2, 1905, TR MSS; TR to Lodge, May 15, 1905, Lodge MSS; TR to Spring Rice, May 13, 1905, and Taft to TR, April 5, 1905, TR MSS.

American public, Baron Kaneko reported to Tokyo. He cabled in January 1905 that Henry Adams advised exorbitant demands which one could reduce. "As Russian peasants can never pay taxes unless whipped by collectors," Adams said, so the Russian government "will never yield to Japan's demands unless forced."[28] Later Kaneko reported that Captain Mahan at a dinner in New York had favored control over Dalny, the Manchurian railway, and even Manchuria.[29]

The most specific sounding of American opinion was still to come. Barnabas Tokutaro Sakai, a Harvard graduate and owner of a Christian hotel for students at the University of Tokyo, was serving as the right-hand man of Kaneko on the publicity mission. In early October 1904 he had written an old friend, Anson Phelps Stokes, then the secretary of Yale University, "What is the feeling or sentiment among the learned scholars in New Haven as to what terms of peace Japan should make etc.? What do you think about it yourself? I should like to hear it from you sometime. We are in constant touch with home through wire." Stokes saw the request as serious, and replied that he would consult two or three Yale professors.[30] Stokes wrote letters to Theodore S. Woolsey, professor of international law, and F. Wells Williams—known affectionately to the Yale students as "Oriental Bill," assistant professor of Far Eastern history and the son of Commodore Perry's interpreter on the epochal visit of 1853-1854.[31] Stokes asked for suggestions on peace terms, requested by a Japanese gentleman who had an

28 Takahira to Komura, from Kaneko, Jan. 13, 1905 (#83), Kaneko Reel MT804, Japanese Foreign Ministry Archives.

29 Takahira to Komura, from Kaneko, Jan. 29, 1905 (#3057), Telegram Series, Reels for 1905, Japanese Foreign Ministry Archives.

30 Barnabas Sakai to Anson Phelps Stokes, Oct. 3, 1904, and Stokes to Sakai, Oct. 7, 1904, Anson Phelps Stokes MSS in Yale University Library.

31 Stokes to F. Wells Williams and Theodore S. Woolsey, Oct. 7, 1904, Stokes MSS.

influential position in his government. After consulting Williams, Woolsey answered. The professors said they could not speak for American public opinion or even the Yale faculty, but could give individual views, not in any way for publication.

Woolsey suggested that the Japanese keep principles in mind while drawing up their peace demands. Russian conduct justified a guarantee as to future action; the war had been an act of self-defense on Japan's part and the Japanese should avoid having to do their work again; they had earned a paramount position in Korea; they should help train Chinese troops to protect a restored Manchuria; commerce of all powers was to be guaranteed in Manchuria and Korea. The professors suggested that the Japanese with these principles should demand that the Russians limit the Asiatic fleet, confirm China's title to Manchuria, transfer Port Arthur, allow control over Korea, surrender all Russian vessels in neutral ports. There should be no indemnity, although the Russians were to turn over railroad property, and no cession of Siberian territory such as Vladivostok, for it would excite the resistance of the Russians.[32] If the Japanese demanded an indemnity they might hold Vladivostok temporarily, so Woolsey suggested.

Stokes agreed, and in mid-October forwarded the professors' suggestion to Sakai.[33] Sakai acknowledged this letter as a valuable piece of advice. He would send it to his government and was sure the government would find it of use. Sakai wrote again two weeks later, thanking Stokes and the professors: "The interest with which you and the other gentlemen have tried to help our Government in dealing with one of the most intricate problems

[32] Woolsey to Stokes, Oct. 14, 1904 (#1580), Kaneko Reel MT804, Japanese Foreign Ministry Archives and Stokes MSS.

[33] Stokes to Sakai, Oct. 14, 1904 (#1580), Kaneko Reel MT804, Japanese Foreign Ministry Archives and Stokes MSS.

is greatly appreciated by us, and I am sure that those clear, far-sighted and important statements which you have sent to me will receive most careful consideration when Japan shall terminate the war." He noted that Kaneko, planning a speaking engagement at Yale, had read the terms and felt under a great obligation to Stokes.[34]

After the fall of Port Arthur in January 1905 Sakai wrote Stokes that the gist of the letter of October 14 had gone to Tokyo by cable at the cost of thousands of dollars—this was untrue, for Kaneko did not send the Yale suggestions to Tokyo until February 12, 1905.[35] Sakai asked if the Yale friends had any modifications to suggest as a result of the changed fortunes of war. He said that Kaneko had shown the Yale suggestions to President Roosevelt. The professors did not have changes, except to limit the Japanese retention of Port Arthur. Woolsey added, and Stokes agreed, that he had no objection to a moderate indemnity, but Williams opposed. This reply went to Japan.[36] Sakai later wrote Stokes that Kaneko had sent it with much appreciation.[37]

Here was the so-called Yale Symposium. Despite Takahira's statement to Secretary Hay that his government did not approve Kaneko's inviting the faculty of Yale to give views on the peace—which was an example of the jealousy between Takahira and Kaneko and brought an angry defense from the baron—the symposium showed

[34] Sakai to Stokes, Oct. 21 and 25, and Nov. 8, 1904, Stokes MSS.

[35] Takahira to Komura, from Kaneko, Feb. 12, 1905 (#3067), Telegram Series, Reels for 1905, Japanese Foreign Ministry Archives.

[36] Sakai to Stokes, Feb. 9, 1905, Stokes MSS; Kaneko to TR, Feb. 9, 1905, TR MSS; Stokes to Sakai, Feb. 10, 1905, and Stokes to Woolsey, Feb. 11, 1905, Stokes MSS; Woolsey to Stokes, Feb. 12, 1905 (#1588), Kaneko Reel MT804, Japanese Foreign Ministry Archives and Stokes MSS; Stokes to Sakai, Feb. 13, 1905 (#1589), Kaneko Reel MT804, Japanese Foreign Ministry Archives and Stokes MSS; Takahira to Komura, Feb. 12, 1905 (#3067), and Takahira to Komura, Feb. 21, 1905 (#3075), Telegram Series, Reels for 1905, Japanese Foreign Ministry Archives.

[37] Sakai to Stokes, Feb. 14, 1905, Stokes MSS.

what demands the American public would accept.[38] Sakai afterward said that Kaneko and Komura had found the statements useful. The suggestion of the professors was discovered years later in the private stationery box of the Japanese emperor.[39]

Komura in early April 1905 decided to base his country's requirements on two principles: hold everything won up to that point and use it as the opportunity permitted; seek peace as quickly as possible, continuing friendly relations with foreign powers to prevent combinations against Japanese interests. The cabinet discussed peace on April 21 but reached no decision. After meetings in June of the elder statesmen *(genro)*, cabinet ministers, and high military and naval officials, the government decided its position in a meeting on July 4 at the residence of Katsura. Attending were four *genro* (Ito, Aritomo Yamagata, Kaoru Inouye, Masayoshi Matsukata) together with Katsura, Komura, War Minister Terauchi, and Navy Minister Gonnohyoei Yamamoto. Next day the conditions of peace received the imperial sanction and appeared in instructions to the chief plenipotentiary Komura. Less severe than those suggested in 1904, these terms consisted of three groups.[40] The first were indispensable and guaranteed the position the Japanese had gained in the war: control of Korea, Russian withdrawal of troops from Manchuria, cession of rights in the Liaotung peninsula and the railway south of Harbin. Second were the relatively important terms: indemnity, transfer of Russian war vessels in neutral ports, Sakhalin and adjoining islands, fishing rights in Russian territorial waters. The third group was for the discretion of the plenipoten-

38 Hay Diary, Feb. 20, 1905, Hay MSS; and Takahira to Komura, from Kaneko, Feb. 21, 1905 (#3075), Telegram Series, Reels for 1905, Japanese Foreign Ministry Archives.

39 Sakai to Stokes, March 17, 1934, and Sept. 27, 1934, Stokes MSS.

40 Gaimusho, *Komura Gaikoshi,* II, 33-34.

tiaries: limitation of Russian naval strength in the Far East, and conversion of Vladivostok to a commercial port by leveling its fortifications.

Comparison of these terms handed Komura and those prepared by the foreign minister in August 1904 shows how pressing Japanese internal problems had become by the summer of 1905. There were fewer indispensable terms, leaving the delegates the right to sacrifice demands. The indemnity and cession of Sakhalin received lower priority; the government did not mention the 1904 demands for access to the Amur River towns as well as use of the Chinese Eastern railway. Russian ships in the Far East, delivery of interned vessels to the Japanese, the conversion of Vladivostok to a commercial port, while new points of discussion had a low priority. The naval demands also showed less concern for the open door in China.

Meanwhile the government attempted to assure Komura of the major military and financial preliminaries to a satisfactory peace negotiation. These were the defeat of the Russian army under its new commander, N. P. Linievich, and the crushing of hope for a Russian comeback in Manchuria; driving Russian troops out of North Korea; the capture of Sakhalin; and a new foreign loan amounting to 292 million yen. The first was impossible, since the Japanese were not strong enough to venture much farther than Mukden. The loan, while difficult, was possible and in July an emergency imperial ordinance called for another loan in London; the subscription filled because of the prospect of peace. As for driving the Russians from North Korea, that was a fact, which left only occupation of Sakhalin to Japanese strategy prior to the conference.

Sakhalin was a different item. The idea of occupying the island was not new, for General Nagaoka, who replaced General Gentaro Kodama as vice chief-of-staff in June 1904, had advocated it; but neither the army nor the navy was in favor. Komura saw its importance. The Supreme War Council in March 1905 had issued orders for the capture of Sakhalin, but by this time the Baltic fleet was in the Far East and Sakhalin had to wait. While Tokyo and Washington were negotiating after Tsushima, Komura and Ito talked the general staff into occupying Sakhalin to obtain a diplomatic advantage at the conference. The occupation of Sakhalin began on July 7 amid Russian threats to boycott the conference, with the landing at Korsakov of the Thirteenth Division commanded by Major General Haraguchi. The Japanese completed this operation before the conference.[41]

One other factor increased the bargaining position of the Japanese. In late March 1905 the Japanese and the British began discussions for a renewal of their alliance. The negotiations had a changed character, for no longer was there a guarantee of Korean independence. The British saw the Japanese as having paramount interests in Korea that extended to political, military, and economic affairs. The terms of the alliance's renewal would not become public but strengthened the determination to force demands on Russia.

With the preparations, diplomatic and military, and assurance by Griscom that "not one member or attaché of the Japanese peace delegation or any one else connected with the Japanese Government will be asked a question or required to make a statement of any kind by the immigration authorities," chief plenipotentiary Komura and his party on July 8 left for the conference from Shimbashi station in Tokyo.[42] The delegation received an impressive

41 *Ibid.*, 34-38.

42 TR to Griscom, June 19, 1905, and Griscom to TR, June 19, 1905, TR MSS.

sendoff by a crowd estimated at 5,000—exuberant on account of victories and, not knowing the delicate internal situation, the substantial terms that were expected. Present were several princes of the Imperial family; Katsura and other cabinet members; *genros* such as Ito, Yamagata, Inouye, and Matsukata; Princes Tokugawa, Shimazu, and Kujo; members of both houses of the Diet; as well as military and naval representatives of Imperial headquarters; businessmen; foreign and diplomatic personages. Komura was aware of the possible failure of his mission. He did not believe he could gain a peace acceptable to the uninformed public, and told Katsura that when he returned his popularity would probably be slight. The aged Count Inouye told Komura he was in a most difficult position as chief Japanese plenipotentiary and that past honor and achievements might disappear. Ito assured Komura that he if no one else would be at the pier to receive him back after the Portsmouth meeting.[43] Komura and group left Shimbashi on three reserved railway cars for the short trip to Yokohama, where they departed for the United States on the Great Northern Steamship Company's liner *Minnesota,* which raised the Japanese flag in the foreign minister's honor. James J. Hill, the American railway magnate, owned the ship and arranged Komura's passage as he was to arrange the trip from the West Coast to New York. Hill was interested in commerce in the Far East.

The trip through the United States took, of course, several days. On arrival in Seattle on July 19 Komura met a crowd of 3,000, including the mayor, and toured the city under police escort.[44] The shops noticeably had closed. Enthusiastic crowds waved hats and handkerchiefs, a surprising reception for a representative of the yellow

[43] Gaimusho, *Komura Gaikoshi,* II, 40-41.
[44] New York *Times,* July 21, 1905.

peril: Americans did not wish to live with Japanese but hoped that Komura would gain victories at the conference. Komura reached New York to find a gala reception, an Italian band met him as he left the ferry. At a reception at the Japan Club he and Kaneko met the rest of the delegation: Minister Takahira, Aimaro Sato, Yenjiro Yamaza, Colonel Koichiro Tachibana; Mineichiro Adachi; Henry W. Denison.[45]

[45] *Ibid.*, July 26 and 27, 1905.

Chapter Six

ROOSEVELT AND THE RUSSIANS

It cannot be said that the cause of reform, advocated by about one million out of a people of 140 millions, has much chance of success. But what is certain is that the whole fabric of society is falling, and that disorders are increasing.[1]

THERE WAS something strange about the president of the United States lecturing the Russians on the need to make peace and warning of a possible collapse of the Romanov dynasty. The Russians had declined from the great days of Alexander I, the victory over Napoleon, and the Holy Alliance. The prestige of the empire had diminished throughout the whole nineteenth century. The tsar now was Nicholas II, weak, indecisive, unpopular, surrounded by self-seeking advisers. Because of the decline of the empire the president of a young country across the Pacific was talking to the ruler of a nation whose history went back a thousand years. The Russian emperor was listening.

Roosevelt's well-founded belief that Russian collapse was possible was based primarily on reports from Meyer. Some comments on Meyer as an observer are in order. While in Rome, Meyer had made the American embassy popular and influential. He formed contacts with European aristocracy, for Meyer with his Boston background represented the best of American society. As a result he was able to gain access to Russian society upon arrival in St. Petersburg and to gather information that was often accurate and revealing. But such contacts, combined with Meyer's own conservative outlook and prejudices, brought acceptance of certain views. Meyer accepted monarchy as the natural form of government for Russia. He was shocked at the manner with which the Russian government was run—its backwardness, inefficiency, and corruption—but came to lay most of the blame on the bureaucracy, not on the tsar. Meyer's sources of information made it difficult for him to see the basic troubles of the country. Much of his information came from the diplomatic corps, frequently dining with other diplomats. In particular he saw a lot of the British, both Ambassador Charles Hardinge and First Secretary Cecil Spring Rice. Another source was the social circles of St. Petersburg, and Meyer came to know many members of the Russian aristocracy, learning much information from them.

Meyer seemed to use "socialist," "revolutionist," and other such terms rather loosely, even after his arrival in St. Petersburg. An examination of his correspondence reveals a tendency to divide antigovernment feelings into two groups—the "revolutionists" and the "reformers." It is doubtful that Meyer came to an understanding of the differences between the Social Revolutionaries and the Social Democrats (both Mensheviks and Bolsheviks). If he did, it is not discussed in his correspondence to Washington. He did, of course, see the great difference between these parties on one hand, and the Kadets and Octobrists on the other. The distinction in his mind was between those who favored reforms while keeping the monarchy (the latter two) and those who wanted to tear down the government.[2]

[1] Spring Rice to Mrs. Roosevelt, March 13, 1905, TR MSS.

[2] See the letters from Meyer to TR on the following dates: Jan. 28, Feb. 21, March 5 and 25, April 13 and 24, May 1, 5, 10, and 16, June 5, 9, and 18, July 1, 8, 18, and Aug. 1 and 9, 1905, in the TR MSS; see also Meyer to Hay on May 23 and 31, and June 21, 1905, Hay MSS; and

While the new ambassador perhaps did not understand the causes of the trouble, his letters to Roosevelt and other correspondents were a clear account. From his arrival in early April, he watched the domestic situation, talking with people. His discussion with diplomats, officials, and nobles led to uncovering the "real history" of Bloody Sunday, that tragic January day which marked the beginning of the Revolution of 1905. He discovered that officials had encouraged labor unions, which got beyond control and accepted the leadership of Father George Gapon. Workmen hoped to carry to the tsar a petition listing the grievances that had led to a strike at the Putilov Works in St. Petersburg. Meyer said that only the pathetic trust of the people made them think they might "lay their petition at his feet." The petition was in the hands of the government before the march. To approach the square before the Winter Palace where the marchers hoped to find the tsar, they had to cross the Neva River by three bridges, which troops could have occupied, not allowing the crowd to assemble. Like everything the Russians did, they awoke to the situation too late, and blundered.[3] The marchers, many of whom were carrying sacred icons and portraits of the tsar, were ordered to halt and disperse, and when they refused the troops fired on

---

Spring Rice to Mrs. Roosevelt on Feb. 15, March 13 and 29, April 26, May 23, 1905, TR MSS.

Meyer was not alone in his misunderstanding of the Russian political situation. Indeed his reports were typical of those sent to Paris by Maurice Bompard, to London by Hardinge, to Berlin by Friederich Johann von Alvensleben, and to Vienna by Aloys Lexa von Aehrenthal. Two good articles revealing the feelings of diplomats are A. Ascher, "The Coming Storm: The Austro-Hungarian Embassy on Russia's Internal Crisis, 1902-1906," *Survey: A Journal of Soviet and East European Studies,* LIII (1964); and René Girault, "Le révolution russe de 1905 d'après quelques témoignages français," *Revue historique,* CCXXX (1963). See also the standard collections of diplomatic documents cited elsewhere in this study.

[3] Meyer to TR, January 28 and April 24, 1905, TR MSS.

them. The official estimate, believed low, was 130 killed and several hundred wounded.

Meyer wrote of the staggering effect of this slaughter. The people had lost their trust in the tsar and were "ripe for socialistic agitations." The strike continued, and so did agitation for constitutional reforms. The spirit of revolution seemed to be awakening, for Nicholas appeared unmindful of the people. The emperor received selected workmen and listened to grievances, but it was too late. The opponents of the tsar united: workers, peasants, revolutionaries, students, liberals, even members of the nobility. The strike grew and the *zemstvos* (the Russian municipal and provincial assemblies) pressed for reform. The general strike in St. Petersburg led to strikes in other cities—Moscow, Saratov, Ekaterinoslav, Riga, Lodz, Warsaw, and Wilna. Peasant revolts began in the provinces of Kursk, Orel, and Chernigov, and extended to central and northwest Russia. Meyer also commented on the assassination in early February of the Grand Duke Sergei Aleksandrovich, governor-general of Moscow and the tsar's uncle and brother-in-law, by a bomb thrown into his carriage by an expelled student: "It is a rather strange coincidence that in order to kill reform and progress of intelligent men, the Grand Duke Serge brought about the formation of labor unions, which caused the memorable disturbance and indirectly brought on his own destruction."[4]

The ambassador observed unrest and uncertainty upon his arrival in St. Petersburg. In his initial letter to the president he said that despite the outward pomp—at his first audience with the emperor, held at Tsarskoe Selo, he drove from the station to the palace in a gilded coach with six white horses—affairs of state were not in order.

[4] *Ibid.*

The people of St. Petersburg were more concerned with internal affairs than with the war in the Far East. The movement for reform was gaining momentum, even the lower clergy were in revolt against the ineptness, arbitrariness, and tyranny of the hierarchy. Three thousand doctors imitated other professional people by forming a national league to struggle for administrative reform of the bureaucracy and to promote representative government. People had little faith in any serious reform by the present government and thus the tendency was toward organization. Few diplomats in St. Petersburg thought the revolutionaries could succeed. The government had troops stationed near the cities. But if the troops turned revolutionary, Meyer believed the situation would become quite different. The government was following a policy of drift and postponements, and the people realized it was a matter of words with the government, not action: "It is very sad to see this country drifting towards chaos from a lack of appreciation of the real situation and the necessity of reforms." The effect was that the Russian government had to fight a two-front war —the Japanese in the Far East and the Russian people throughout the empire. A decisive defeat by either seemed to hold disaster for the monarchy in Russia.[5]

Meyer's pessimism increased as he described conditions at the end of April 1905. The ship of state drifted, no one at the helm. Many promises for reform, nothing accomplished. The tsar's mind, the ambassador said, was like a pendulum. In defeat he considered the internal affairs of the country and appointed a commission to report at some future date what had to be done. If military victory seemed possible, as during the voyage of the Baltic fleet, the possibility drove away other considera-

[5] Meyer Diary, April 16, 1905, Meyer MSS LC; Meyer to TR, April 13, 1905, TR MSS; and Meyer to Thomas Meyer, April 16, 1905, Meyer MSS.

tions. As bad a leader as was the tsar, Meyer thought the government worse. He reported the extent of army disorganization inconceivable. He reported that Kuropatkin had lost two thirds of his war maps including those of the fortifications of Vladivostok. A Swedish military attaché on the Russian side in the battle of Mukden termed the confusion and rout of the Russian army indescribable. Many officers fled as far as Tieling and there proceeded to get drunk.[6]

As April passed Meyer discovered that the revolutionary movement included people of nearly every social class, even the high nobility. One day a reform was announced, the next day annulled, "due to the influence of the last minister who may have seen His Majesty." The idea of representative government, Meyer wrote, was permeating all classes.[7]

Meyer wrote of the prevarications, misrepresentations, and procrastinations of the bureaucracy. The emperor no sooner had made an advance in the right direction than the bureaucracy weakened the step by a communication to the press or by dilatory tactics. A recent example was Nicholas's meeting on June 19 with a committee of fourteen, in which he declared his intention to summon a representative assembly and said, "I hope from this day forward that the relations between me and my people will enter a new phase." When printed, this was modified to represent less advanced ideas. A St. Petersburg journal, *Rus,* was suppressed for a month for printing a *zemstvo* address the tsar had received, which the bureaucracy considered an illegal document passed and adopted by an unauthorized gathering. Meyer compared the emperor to a weak but honest mayor in New York City, with Tammany Hall in control, the difference being

[6] Meyer to TR, April 24, 1905, TR MSS.
[7] Meyer to TR, May 1 and 16, 1905, TR MSS.

that the tsar could remove anyone without reasons or excuses, but unfortunately lacked the forcefulness. The ambassador continued, "Yet I believe his intentions are honest and well-meant, but he is surrounded by men who are not in sympathy with needed reform, nor are they to be relied upon."[8]

The Russian government, so Meyer reported, had split over the war. Many opposed the tsar's decision for the peace conference. They declared that the Japanese had reached the peak of their power, while the Russian military was just getting into stride. Troops arriving in the Far East were first-class, and communications problems of the early part of the war were solved. More and more pressure was placed upon the tsar in June and July. If the Japanese were strong, many asked, why were they inactive on the battlefield? Others desired peace to calm the country, but they too saw conditions as unacceptable. Both sides struggled to convince the tsar. Meyer reported that the tsar was in favor of continuing the war.[9]

All this convinced Roosevelt that the tsar was "in a thoroughly Chinese mood." If Nicholas refused to do anything, the president felt that the emperor's blood was on his own hands. Fearing a collapse and Japanese dominance in the Far East, Roosevelt spent much energy in June and July 1905 trying to convince the Russians of the need for peace at almost any cost. The best statement of the hopes of the American president appeared in a letter to Henry Cabot Lodge in mid-June 1905.[10] After discussing the diplomacy connected with getting the Russians and the Japanese to agree to a conference, which had convinced Roosevelt of "the utterly loose way in which the Russian Government works," he told of his

[8] Meyer to TR, June 18 and July 1, 1905, TR MSS; and Meyer to Hay, June 21, 1905, Hay MSS.

[9] Meyer to TR, June 5, 9, and 18, July 1, 8, and 18, 1905, TR MSS.

[10] TR to Lodge, June 5 and 16, 1905, Lodge MSS.

attempts to convince the tsar of peace and the reasons he desired it. He had not been content to advise through the American ambassador; realizing the help Wilhelm rendered in getting the tsar's agreement for Portsmouth, the president had decided to enlist German support. He instructed Ambassador Tower to thank the kaiser for all he had done. The ambassador was to state that the kaiser's aid might force the tsar to conclude peace. Roosevelt hoped the Japanese would be moderate and had so asked them himself. The tsar had to understand that the Japanese were the victors and now had nothing to fear from the Russians. The Russians had to make up their minds that the war was a failure, and while they should secure peace on the best possible terms they should get it at all hazards. Roosevelt earnestly hoped the kaiser would advise Russia to look at this matter from the standpoint of commonsense.[11] If there followed no action from Berlin, the kaiser wanted peace and when the time came would do all he could to bring it.

Roosevelt frequently consulted the Russian ambassador —Cassini, and then Rosen—calling for acceptance of whatever demands the Japanese made. With the arrival of Rosen on July 4, the president talked of a subject "which evidently preoccupied his mind most earnestly—the success of the coming Peace Conference."[12] Rosen attempted to controvert the president's belief that peace was a matter of necessity for the Russians. Rosen said that the position in Manchuria was not at all hopeless because two army corps, some of the best Russian troops from the western frontier, were on their way; no serious Japanese advance had taken place since Mukden; the Japanese could only spare the small number of troops needed to occupy Sak-

[11] TR to Tower, June 24, 1905, SDA NA.

[12] Roman Rosen, *Forty Years of Diplomacy*, 2 vols. (New York, 1922), I, 260.

halin, after the Russians consented to negotiations for peace.

Roosevelt told Meyer to continue to urge peace. He thought the disaster to the Russians would be so great that the country would cease to count among major powers for a generation to come, unless "as foreshadowed in your last letter, there is a revolution which makes her count as the French did after their revolution."[13] Some of Meyer's friends among the nobility had returned from their country places, no longer safe as the unrest spread to rural Russia. The condition of the Black Sea fleet was lamentable and if the mutiny that appeared in the navy spread to the army, he thought the dynasty doomed. What was needed, Meyer decided, was a regime of discussion, action, publicity, not one of mystery, inaction, and duplicity.[14]

There was a note of hope in Meyer's letter. Rebellion of Russian marines at Libau and the Black Sea fleet mutiny at Odessa finally made some officials see peace as a necessity. The last mobilization of troops had proved so unpopular that it was discontinued in St. Petersburg and many men were sent back home. There was even a meeting of ministers presided over by the tsar which actually "accomplished something, spurred on, and even alarmed, by the effect that had been produced throughout the country by the discussions of the Moscow conference [of *zemstvo* leaders]." The ministers voted in favor of the tsar's granting a constitution and convening a national assembly. The ministers of foreign affairs, justice, court, and agriculture all opposed such measures—they naturally dreaded the power of interrogation which the assembly would have. The minister of finance and public instruction refrained from voting. D. F. Trepov, gover-

[13] TR to Meyer, July 7, 1905, Meyer MSS.
[14] Meyer to TR, July 8, 1905, TR MSS.

nor-general of St. Petersburg, surprised everyone by voting for the national assembly and appearing for the first time as a reformer. Meyer thought Trepov the best-informed man in Russia on internal conditions. Clearly, Trepov saw the need for reform. Others warned Nicholas that unless the national assembly was called and other reforms were granted, they considered the Romanov dynasty in real danger of being overthrown. The speeches seemed to make a deep impression on the tsar. Meyer hoped Nicholas would make peace and grant reforms before it was too late.[15]

But *Novoe Vremya* said the Russians could only consent to a peace that would not affect the dignity or interest of the empire.[16] In a tone characteristic of Cassini the newspaper insisted that "our plenipotentiaries must remember that they must defend the interests not only of Russians but also of other Caucasian powers and they will find moral support in Berlin, Paris, Washington and perhaps even in London."

Then came a surprise. Thousands of miles from Washington, the kaiser and the tsar in the formality of a pageant concluded a treaty aboard their yachts on the Bay of Björkö in the Baltic Sea. The Treaty of Björkö, if carried out, would have meant an alliance between Germany and Russia, shattering diplomatic arrangements then prevailing in Europe, with incalculable meaning for the Far East. Roosevelt breathed a sigh of relief when he found out that the tsar's ministers had refused to accept it.

Only with difficulty did the Russians see that they could not win the war. They had entered the conflict—rather, stumbled into it—with no diplomatic goals or

15 Meyer to TR, August 9, 1905, TR MSS.

16 *Novoe Vremya,* July 17, 1905, as cited in Portsmouth *Daily Chronicle,* July 18, 1905.

military strategy. After the war began they remained confident of victory and gave no thought to the necessity of accepting Japanese demands.[17] Only after Port Arthur, Mukden, and Tsushima did the Russian government begin to see that peace was necessary. After the Japanese triumphs of 1905 even the most staunch believer in the Russian army saw that the Japanese had the upper hand. Peasant disorders also were on the rise. Finally there was finance. At the time of his departure for the United States, Witte reported that there was not the slightest hope of floating either a domestic or a foreign loan. The Russians could continue the war only by resorting to new issues of paper money, that is, by preparing the way for a complete financial and consequently economic collapse.[18]

In early July 1905 the minister of finance, Kokovtsov, noted it was not necessary to seek peace at any price; if such was the case the Russian delegates would not need instructions. Kokovtsov did admit that it was to Russia's interest financially to conclude peace, but war or peace could not be decided from a financial standpoint. He believed the negotiators should only seek the Japanese terms. Any conditions the Russians accepted, he hoped, would lead to a just peace and no mere armistice. Plenipotentiaries should avoid terms that would endanger Russian possessions. The minister thought that an indemnity could be avoided by the surrender of certain railways to China which would pay a redemption price to Japan. Beyond this the Russians should consider no indemnity. Finally the Russians should recognize Japan's dominant interest in Korea—though the Japanese should keep no forces or fortifications in the area—and demand

17 Hardinge to Lansdowne, June 30, 1904 (#3), *British Documents on the Origins of the War, 1898-1914,* 11 vols. (London, 1926-1938), IV.

18 Sergei Witte, *Vospominaniia* [Memoirs], 3 vols. (Moscow, 1960), II, 400-401.

protection of private rights of Russian subjects in areas surrendered to the Japanese.[19]

Incredible as the above terms might seem, considering the defeats, Kokovtsov was not alone in his opinion. Lieutenant General Pavel F. Unterberger, governor-general of Amur province, not only agreed but thought that such terms as surrender of Sakhalin, turning Vladivostok into a commercial port, and limitation of Russian naval forces in Far Eastern waters were completely unacceptable.[20] Like Kokovtsov he did not think the Russians were in a position that called for peace at any terms. He opposed every sort of indemnity. The argument that a continued war would mean the loss of Far Eastern possessions was not valid, for even if the Japanese did capture Siberia the area would be of no economic advantage. The cost of Japanese military occupation of Siberia would be ruinous.

With these opinions, and others, Lamsdorff set about preparing a report to the emperor requesting instruction on all questions that the Japanese would bring to the conference. His report dealt with Korea where, the foreign minister stated, the Russians had to renounce their claims and abandon all hope of influence. The report turned to the matter of an indemnity, stating that the Japanese would demand one; but Lamsdorff did not express his views on this subject. It mentioned a limit on Russian military force in the Far East, but again Lamsdorff offered no clear ideas.[21]

The emperor returned this report to the foreign min-

19 Lamsdorff to Kokovtsov, June 29, 1905 (#53), and Kokovtsov to Lamsdorff, July 3, 1905 (#56), *Sbornik diplomaticheskikh dokumentov* and *Krasnyi arkhiv* [Red Archives], 106 vols. (Moscow, 1922-1941) VI, 13-17: see also V. N. Kokovtsov, *Out of My Past* (Stanford, 1935), 54-56.

20 Pavel Unterberger to Kokovtsov, June 9, 1905, *Krasnyi arkhiv,* VI, 9-12.

21 Kokovtsov, *Out of My Past,* 54-55. For other opinions, see War Minister to Lamsdorff, July 1, 1905 (#54), and Navy Minister to Lamsdorff, July 4, 1905 (#57), *Sbornik diplomaticheskikh dokumentov.*

ister in a short time with marginal notations. At the head of the report the tsar wrote, "I am ready to terminate by peace a war which I did not start, provided the conditions offered us befit the dignity of Russia. I do not consider that we are beaten; our army is still intact, and I have faith in it." The emperor was willing to make peace but not on any terms. On each subject the tsar's instructions were clear. Next to the section of the report discussing Korea the emperor noted, "On this subject I am ready to make concessions; this is not Russian territory." Concerning an indemnity the tsar commented, "Russia has never paid an indemnity; I shall never consent to this," and he underlined the word *never* three times. On the last subject—limitation of Russian forces in the Far East—Nicholas wrote, "This is not to be thought of; we are not beaten; we can continue the war if unacceptable terms should force us to it."[22]

The emperor on July 12 approved Witte's final instructions based on these ideas. Concessions too close to national dignity included surrender of Russian territory; an indemnity; dismantlement of fortifications in Vladivostok; a limit of Russian naval forces in the Far East; surrender of the railroad connecting Vladivostok and the rest of Siberia; any other limit of Russian freedom in the Pacific. Russian delegates had arguments and alternatives, should the Japanese insist. To a demand for indemnity Witte was to suggest financial or commercial concessions such as tariff privileges on the Siberian and Chinese Eastern railroads. To demands for Sakhalin, Witte was to point out the historic and economic importance of the island. The Russians were ready to recognize Japan's position in Korea, although Korea was to remain independent. The Japanese were not to introduce troops in North Korea nor to construct fortifications and had to

22 *Ibid.*, 55.

assure passage in the Korean strait. Russian delegates could agree to transfer the Kwantung peninsula, as well as Port Arthur and Dalny, but the Chinese had to approve. With similar approval Russia would cede the South Manchuria railway up to the border of Kirn province.[23] These demands contrasted with those the Japanese had prepared, and indicated that negotiations at the Portsmouth conference were to be difficult.

Witte himself had ideas about peace. In 1904, as noted, he had called for victory and believed Russian dominance in the Far East would be assured only with the absorption of Manchuria and Korea.[24] By 1905 he had changed his views, and in March told Ambassador Hardinge that the Russians should get the best possible terms from the Japanese, but should pull out of Manchuria, recognize Korea under Japanese influence, cede Port Arthur with the Liaotung peninsula and the railway to Harbin, and even agree to keep Russian warships out of Chinese waters. While opposing an indemnity he saw no objection to making Vladivostok an open port.[25] In July, Hardinge again reported to London. Witte continued to oppose an indemnity and cession of territory; he thought that the character of the Russian mind ruled such conditions impossible. The first plenipotentiary hoped to bring a discussion of all issues between Tokyo and St. Petersburg, possibly preparing the way for friendly relations in the future.[26]

Publicly Witte's statements were less compromising.

[23] Instructions to Witte, July 12, 1905 (#65), and instructions to N. V. Muraviev, July 11, 1905 (#60), *Sbornik diplomaticheskikh dokumentov.*

[24] Hardinge to Lansdowne, June 30, 1904 (#3), *British Documents on the Origins of the War, 1898-1914,* IV.

[25] Hardinge to Lansdowne, July 15, 1905 (#88), *British Documents on the Origins of the War, 1898-1914,* IV. In this letter Hardinge reminds Lansdowne of a conversation he had reported before the Russians had accepted Roosevelt's mediation.

[26] Hardinge to Lansdowne, July 24, 1905 (#89), *British Documents on the Origins of the War, 1898-1914,* IV.

He was quoted as saying that his appointment did not indicate the Russians wished peace at any price. He was going to work as best he could, but feared that Japanese terms would be such that he would be unable to accept them. He noted two parties—those in favor of war at any price, and those (to which he belonged) who favored peace so long as demands did not wound the amour propre of the Russian people or jeopardize Russia's national future. If Japanese terms were moderate, why not announce them before the conference? To this he added, to the astonishment of most who had followed the war and internal Russian conditions, that Russia was not crushed. He admitted that the internal situation was serious, but said that the significance of what was happening had been misunderstood. Russia had little resemblence to western countries, and to know Russia one had to understand the soul of the Russian people. Russia, Witte said, could not be judged by western standards because its customs, history, and peoples were different. While possessing an immense country the Russian people were a great family. At present they were torn by internal differences, but the divisions would disappear if the integrity and future of the country were at stake. Russia was passing through a crisis and would shortly again take its place as a preponderant power in the European arena.[27]

As plenipotentiary, Witte decided upon a strategy and spent much of his trip to the United States working on it. He left St. Petersburg on July 19 for Paris where he wanted to inquire about loans as well as to discover the French attitude toward an indemnity which he felt was the most important issue at the conference. President Emile Loubet and Foreign Minister Maurice Rouvier advised him to be conciliatory. The Russians should not

[27] Portsmouth *Daily Chronicle,* July 19, 1905; and the New York *Times,* July 18, 1905.

rely upon Paris for future war loans and should make peace even at the cost of an indemnity, which the French would help to raise. Witte was adamant. When the French president reminded him of the indemnity in 1871, Witte emphasized that circumstances were different, for Japanese troops were not nearing Moscow.[28] In Paris his feelings as a Russian patriot were also hurt—a shock, for the French were allies. "The public treated me, the chief plenipotentiary of the autocrat of all the Russias, as a representative of some political nonentity. Some—a slight minority—sympathized with me, others did not conceal their joy at our misfortune; but the majority treated me with complete indifference."[29]

Next stop was Cherbourg from where he planned to sail on July 26 aboard the *Kaiser Wilhelm der Grosse,* the Hamburg Steamship Company's liner. The delegation received a more cordial welcome from a crowd that included Nelidov, ambassador in Paris, and Cassini, now ambassador in Madrid. "A band was playing," Korostovetz wrote, "people were bathing, strolling about, and taking refreshments on the terrace, while waiting for the arrival of the *Kaiser Wilhelm der Grosse*."[30]

Once at sea Witte set to work. He decided on tactics, and determined not to show himself or the Russians in the least anxious to make peace, and to convey "the impression that if His Majesty had consented to the negotiations, it was merely because of the universal desire on the part of all countries to see the war terminated." He believed he should act as befitted the representative of the greatest empire on earth, even though that empire was in a slight difficulty. Because of the influence of the press in America he decided to give newsmen every at-

[28] Sergei Witte, *Vospominaniia,* II, 404-13.
[29] *Ibid.*
[30] *Korostovetz Diary,* July 26, 1905.

tention, always being accessible. Finally he determined "to behave with democratic simplicity and without a shadow of snobbishness," so as to win the sympathy of the Americans, going as far as to woo the Jews in New York—which conduct he stated was in keeping with his opinion on the Jewish problem.[31] Formulating this strategy he received help from his friend E. J. Dillon, the journalist, who assisted with the statement that the Russian plenipotentiary planned to read on arrival.

At sea, Witte played frequent games of shuffleboard, made many friends aboard ship, and even inquired into the mysteries of the cakewalk which a young Brooklyn actress danced for him. He was much amused by the dance, giving the blushing and winded young lady his autograph when she finished.[32]

Disembarkation was an occasion. A flotilla of small vessels met the liner on arrival in Hoboken, including the steamer *Emigrant,* which brought members of the Slavonic colony in New York and flew Russian and American flags.[33] The Slavs were among the first on board. Witte here met Rosen and other members of the peace delegation. To the newsmen Martens read Witte's speech in which he noted that the tsar had appointed delegates as proof of his friendly feelings for the United States. Should Witte's mission prove unproductive, he hoped this evidence of Russian friendship would remain a memorable event.[34]

From Hoboken the delegation with a Secret Service detail went to the St. Regis Hotel on Fifth Avenue in New York City. There the delegates were to spend the few days before the opening of the conference. This

[31] Sergei Witte, *Vospominaniia,* II, 415-16.
[32] New York *Times,* Aug. 3, 1905.
[33] *Korostovetz Diary,* Aug. 2, 1905; see also the New York *Times,* Aug. 3, 1905; and the Portsmouth *Daily Chronicle,* Aug. 4, 1905.
[34] *Korostovetz Diary,* Aug. 2, 1905.

period in New York was a time of intense social activity. For three days Witte toured the city, visiting the Stock Exchange, Tammany Hall, even immigrant sections of the city where he talked with Russian Jews. This was all part of his strategy to win favorable opinion in the United States. The Russian plenipotentiary gave a dinner for members of the Washington embassy, and on the day that he was to journey to Oyster Bay to meet the president he went with the whole delegation to a Russian Orthodox church in New York City, since it was the name day of Empress Dowager Marie Feodorovna. There the senior priest told Witte that a difficult task awaited him. "May God help you and grant you wisdom," the priest continued, "I am sure that you, with your Russian soul, understand and know exactly what is necessary for the good of Russia. You will do all that can be done under present circumstances."[35]

[35] *Korostovetz Diary,* Aug. 3 and 4, 1905; and the New York *Times,* Aug. 4, 1905.

Chapter Seven

DOWN TO BUSINESS

The feeling that peace will not result from the meeting of the Plenipotentiaries at Portsmouth continues. Russia it is thought will not pay an indemnity nor yield Russian territory to Japan. Japan it is thought will demand not only territory but indemnity.[1]

PEACE CONFERENCES have long been of interest to the historian. Not only have conference "battles," so-called, brought a cessation of hostilities but there always is a story or two of the amenities connected with such meetings. Especially in the nineteenth century conferences were notable, equivalent at least to royal weddings, coronations, and funerals. At one place would gather the representatives of the major powers. After daily meetings there would be the heavy banquets and the balls. Such an assemblage is what the people of Portsmouth expected.

President Roosevelt reduced his social commitments in the summer of 1905 and took up residence at Oyster Bay where he determined to receive the plenipotentiaries before the conference. On Long Island, situated on 83 acres of hillside which the President called Sagamore Hill, Roosevelt in 1885 had built the 22-room Victorian-style house. It contained eight fireplaces, and large rooms filled with mementos of travel and adventure. The furniture was simple but solid, so characteristic of Roosevelt's tastes. In the library, off the front entrance, books lined almost every available place. There the president relaxed and read Dickens, Cooper, Huxley, Thackeray, Parkman, McMaster, Rhodes, Henry Adams, Prescott, Motley. There he entertained guests, listened on the telephone to reports from Washington, and dictated thousands of letters to his secretary William Loeb. There he was to do all he could to gain peace in 1905.[2]

The first group of the plenipotentiaries to arrive, and the first the president received, were the Japanese. As Meyer noted in his diary, "the Japanese Plenipotentiaries are already in America & as usual always ahead of the Russians."[3] Komura and Takahira visited Sagamore Hill on July 28. Because of school ties at Harvard and the frequent communication between Washington and Tokyo during the war, a frank discussion was possible. Roosevelt told the Japanese of his concern about the peace talks and warned them to leave room to negotiate. Then Komura read Roosevelt the demands and discussed them. The president thought the demand for disarming Vladivostok was unnecessary, for the Japanese would get the railway between Harbin and Port Arthur. He pointed out that only one of the interned vessels was usable. Finally he turned to the indemnity, saying that the Japanese should be cautious and get the other demands before bringing it up. Komura agreed with most of what the president said, reserving Japan's right to an indemnity. Roosevelt felt it would be better for the Japanese to bargain for the principle of an indemnity, leaving amounts till later. Komura agreed.[4]

Next day the president had further thoughts on the

[1] Meyer Diary, Aug. 10, 1905, Meyer MSS LC.

[2] Hermann Hagedorn, *A Guide to Sagamore Hill* (New York, 1953), 9-48.

[3] Meyer Diary, July 27, 1905, Meyer MSS LC.

[4] Gaimusho [Foreign Ministry], *Komura Gaikoshi* [A History of Komura's Diplomacy], 2 vols. (Tokyo, 1953), II, 42-44; and Komura and Takahira interview with TR, July 28, 1905, "Kaneko Dan to Bei Daitōryō to no kaiken shimatsu," Kaneko Reel MT804, Japanese Foreign Ministry Archives.

indemnity and wrote Komura in care of Kaneko that, while Witte had ruled out such a payment, a recent cable indicated the Russians would consider at least part of the Japanese war expenses. This Komura might accomplish if he would avoid the word *indemnity*. Kaneko and Komura discussed this letter and agreed that such a substitution of terms would be acceptable.[5]

The president received Witte and Rosen on August 4. They went to Oyster Bay by train, since Witte refused to make the journey on the presidential yacht *Mayflower*.[6] Witte was unimpressed by the mansion at Oyster Bay. He thought it similar to the ordinary summerhouse of a landowner of small means.[7] This was the first meeting, and it was all business. Witte presented the president a message in English from the tsar thanking Roosevelt for calling the conference. The emperor in the note warned he had instructed Witte how far Russian concessions could go.[8] Witte defended the weak Russian position and disagreed with Roosevelt that peace was essential for Russia. He displeased the president in the two-and-one-half-hour talk. Roosevelt said privately that Witte impressed him much during the visit, but "by no means altogether pleasantly."[9] To the president the chief Russian delegate appeared more concerned with his own welfare than that of his nation, and seemed cynical and unscrupulous. As Roosevelt was to write later, the Russians acted with Chinese or Byzantine folly by insisting they were not

[5] TR to Kaneko, July 29, 1905, TR MSS; Gaimusho, *Komura Gaikoshi*, II, 42-44; and Kaneko to TR, July 31, 1905, TR MSS.

[6] *Korostovetz Diary*, Aug. 3 and 4, 1905; and the New York *Times*, Aug. 4, 1905.

[7] Sergei Witte, *Vospominaniia*, [Memoirs], 3 vols. (Moscow, 1960), II, 420.

[8] Nicholas to TR, July 18, 1905 (#71), and Witte to Lamsdorff, Aug. 4, 1905 (#75), *Sbornik diplomaticheskikh dokumentov*.

[9] TR to Spring Rice, Nov. 1, 1905, and TR to Trevelyan, Sept. 12, 1905, TR MSS.

vanquished. It was all he could do, the president noted, "not to tell them some straight-forward truths in uncomplimentary language."[10]

Next was the formal introduction of the delegates at Oyster Bay on August 5, the day after the president's talk with Witte. The delegations traveled from New York on separate cruisers—Japanese on the U.S.S. *Tacoma* and the Russians on the U.S.S. *Chattanooga*. The Japanese and Russian military attachés were in their brilliant uniforms and decorations, and the others in frock coats and top hats. The progress of the *Tacoma* and the *Chattanooga* down the East River was marked by the shrieking of sirens and factory whistles, and ships, boats, and yachts encountered hoisted flags by way of salute. The arrival in Oyster Bay was no less impressive. In the beautiful sandy-shored harbor stood the *Galveston, Sylph, Dolphin,* and *Mayflower*. Bands played and guns saluted as the delegates transferred to the *Mayflower* where the reception was to take place.[11]

Roosevelt had appointed Assistant Secretary of State Herbert H. D. Peirce to arrange the ceremonies so there would be no friction. On the question of receiving the envoys at receptions Peirce decided that the arrival date of a delegation in the United States would determine the order of reception. Hence the Japanese boarded the *Mayflower* first. The Russians followed, and were almost involved in an accident. As the launch carrying the Russians made its way through the maze of pleasure craft it tried to round the bow of a sloop, the *Nellie H.* of Brooklyn. "For a minute," the New York *Times* reported,

10 TR to White, Aug. 23, 1905, TR MSS; and Kaneko interview with TR, Aug. 5, 1905, "Kaneko Dan to Bei Daitōryō to no kaiken shimatsu," Kaneko Reel MT804, Japanese Foreign Ministry Archives.

11 Ship logs of the U.S.S. *Mayflower, Tacoma,* and *Dolphin,* Aug. 5, 1905, Navy Department Records, National Archives; see also *Korostovetz Diary,* Aug. 5, 1905; and the New York *Times,* Aug. 6, 1905.

"it looked as though the *Nellie H.* would sink the launch of the Russian envoys. There was a breathless moment of suspense at the close of which the little launch from the *Chattanooga* emerged."[12]

The president led the Russians into a stateroom and there, where the Japanese waited, presented Komura to Witte. Introductions were largely formal, since the Japanese foreign minister knew Witte and Rosen from previous diplomatic assignments (he had met Witte while serving as minister in St. Petersburg, and Rosen had represented the Russians in Tokyo). Witte's secretary, Korostovetz, recorded in his diary that great was the difference between the towering figure of Witte and the small baron. The latter was thin, had a delicate complexion, and looked sickly.[13] After the introductions all slowly moved into the saloon of the *Mayflower* for a cold luncheon. Roosevelt enjoyed the role of host—he spoke to both men at length, to Witte in French and to Komura in English. There were no chairs about the luncheon table, for the president wanted to avoid all offense concerning seating. With champagne in hand he proposed a toast to which there was to be no answer and which the delegates were asked to drink in silence. He toasted the welfare and prosperity of the sovereigns and people of Russia and Japan and said it was his hope and prayer that a just and lasting peace would be speedily concluded.[14]

From Oyster Bay the scene shifted to Portsmouth, and for Roosevelt this meant the end of his official duties. Now he had to go backstage and await the negotiation.

Fog delayed the beginning of the conference in Ports-

[12] New York *Times*, Aug. 6, 1905.

[13] *Korostovetz Diary*, Aug. 5, 1905.

[14] Witte to Lamsdorff, Aug. 7, 1905 (#76), *Sbornik diplomaticheskikh dokumentov;* Komura to Katsura, Aug. 8, 1905 (#13315), Telegram Series, Reels for 1905, Japanese Foreign Ministry Archives; *Korostovetz Diary*, Aug. 5, 1905; and Gaimusho, *Komura Gaikoshi*, II, 51.

mouth. Going by sea as far as Newport, Rhode Island, Witte made the rest of the journey by land. After a luncheon with the commander of the navy yard at Newport, Admiral Chadwick, he proceeded to Boston by special train, shaking hands with the train's engineer at the completion of the trip. He paid a visit to Harvard where he met the president of the university and some professors for lunch at the Colonial Club. As he prepared to leave for Portsmouth the next day he encountered "people of the Jewish type" at the railroad station. Despite pleas of the Secret Service men—Witte referred to them as guardian angels—he stepped to the platform to engage in a lively discussion with these recent émigrés from Russia. They told Witte they did not like the Russian regime, but loved Russia because its soil held the bones of their ancestors and would forever remain their fatherland. They wished the delegate success. He arrived late that evening in Portsmouth and after spending the night made his way the next morning by launch to the *Mayflower* to take part in the welcoming ceremonies. He enjoyed the little meetings with the American public—he admitted to Korostovetz that until arrival in Portsmouth he had only given work to his digestive organs: "it would be interesting to know when my brain will have to act."[15]

The Japanese, following Roosevelt's schedule, proceeded unnoticed by ship to Portsmouth. The arrival of the flotilla from Oyster Bay on the morning of August 8, 1905, was a call for more ceremonies. As the three ships entered the harbor—Japanese on the *Dolphin,* Russians on the *Mayflower,* with the *Galveston* as an escort—Portsmouth was bursting with pride. It was also bustling with people. In addition to delegates and their staffs, Americans acting in official capacities, residents and guests, newsmen had converged on the small New England town.

[15] Witte, *Vospominaniia,* II, 423-24; and *Korostovetz Diary,* Aug. 8, 1905.

Some of the better known were Dillon of the *Daily Telegraph* (London), George W. Smalley, George E. Morrison, and Donald Mackenzie Wallace of the *Times* (London), Salvatore Cortesi, Associated Press correspondent in Rome, Jules Hademann of *Matin* (Paris), Otto Kahn of *Zeitung* (Frankfurt), Boris Suvorin of *Novoe Vremya* (St. Petersburg), R. Onishi of *Jiji Shimbo* (Tokyo), and K. K. Kawakami of *Asahi* (Tokyo).[16]

At about 11:00 A.M. both delegations left their ships and traveled by launch to a dock in the navy yard where Assistant Secretary Peirce and Admiral William W. Mead, commandant of the yard, greeted them, the Japanese first. They went to the peace building and a reception by Governor McLane. After a copious lunch, with plenty of champagne, as Korostovetz recorded, all departed for the Rockingham County Court House and another reception at which the governor was to speak.[17] The parade in open carriages crossed the bridge connecting Maine and New Hampshire and entered a town decorated with flags, banners, and carpets. Thousands crowded the streets, held back by the New Hampshire national guard standing at attention in blue uniforms with yellow leggings. The courthouse, a bright red brick building, had a welcome sign over its entrance. Inside a gaily decorated draped room awaited the dignitaries. The governor received the visitors and extended the hospitality of his state; he hoped that "in this ancient community, where cluster many of the finest traditions of American history," the negotiations would be crowned by a Treaty of Portsmouth.[18]

After the courthouse formalities the delegates reached

[16] Portsmouth *Daily Chronicle*, Aug. 9, 1905.

[17] Ship log of U.S.S. *Dolphin*, Aug. 8, 1905, Navy Department Records, National Archives; *Korostovetz Diary*, Aug. 8, 1905; and the New York *Times*, Aug. 9, 1905.

[18] Portsmouth *Herald*, Aug. 8, 1905.

the Wentworth Hotel where they stayed as guests of the American government. Under the direction of Assistant Secretary Peirce everything was done to make life comfortable.

American food at this time was quite different from European and Oriental, and the chefs were undecided what they should prepare. At the beginning of the conference they prepared many dishes, hoping the delegates would find something to their taste. One menu, from a banquet for newsmen but similar to the food served the delegates, read:

Scotch Broth Clam Chowder
Olives Cucumbers
Boiled Chicken Halibut, Egg Sauce
Pommes Natural
Boiled Ham, and Cabbage
Chicken Pot Pie, with Dumplings
Spaghetti, a la Italian
Compote of Fruit, Wine Sauce
Sirloin of Beef, au Jus
Loin and Leg of Lamb, Mint Sauce
Boiled New Potatoes Mashed Potatoes
Green Corn Butter Beans
Boiled Rice
Boiled Sweet Potatoes
Tapioca Pudding, Cream Sauce
Blueberry Pie Apple Pie
Macaroons Assorted Cake
Maraschino Ice Cream
Mixed Nuts Layer Raisins
Wafer Crackers Assorted Cheese
Coffee[19]

This kind of a repast did not please the Russians. Witte reported that despite dozens of courses the dishes were

[19] *Ibid.*

mostly cold. To him it appeared that the government had ordered hundreds of dishes and stored them before serving. He thought Americans would eat anything. After two or three days he decided to fast on bread and vegetables. Korostovetz recorded after one session that lunch was served as usual. Witte took nothing and just walked around the room. Witte asked Komura and Takahira if they were well and how they liked the food. The Japanese replied that despite the lack of variety they thought they had become used to it and even tried to enjoy it. The Americans never gave up. They filled later menus with boeuf langue et gambou, grouse à l'aspec, truite saumonee, and saumon froid sauce tartare. Komura took sick at the end of the conference, and Witte said it was the food.[20]

There were problems with accommodations. Witte found the bathtub too short and wrenched his ankle. On another occasion the unlucky Russian complained of too strong a light in his room, whereupon the management corrected the situation by installing a large Japanese matted shade.[21]

The daily trip between the hotel and the navy yard was one of the few times the people of Portsmouth saw the delegates. There were three possible ways to cover the four-mile distance. One was by launch, since the Wentworth had a pier; this was the shortest and least public route. Delegates liked to get out and see people, and so they frequently went by auto (the government supplied Pope-Toledo touring cars) or by carriage. Remarkable are the pictures showing these men enjoying trips on the roads around Portsmouth. The delegates, especially the Russians, mingled with guests at the Went-

[20] *Korostovetz Diary,* Aug. 14 and 15, 1905; Witte, *Vospominaniia,* II, 424-28; and Portsmouth *Herald,* Aug. 16, 1905.

[21] O'Laughlin to TR, Aug. 9, 1905, TR MSS; and the New York *Times,* Aug. 9, 1905.

worth. One local newspaper, the *Herald,* reported that while the Japanese only strolled up and down the verandas, the Russians had passed some time in the ladies' billiard room.[22]

So much did Roosevelt leave the early part of the conference to the plenipotentiaries that they had to work out their own schedule. There was no arrangement for meetings. After dinner at the Wentworth on the first night, Witte sent a short note to Komura asking if a preliminary meeting would be convenient the next morning, August 9. The two delegates arranged for 11 o'clock.[23]

To this first session Witte brought the Russian credentials, but Komura had forgotten his. They agreed to delay the exchange until the next morning, deciding also to meet twice a day, at 9:30 and 3:00, with each session lasting about three hours. Not so easily settled was who would take part. Witte hoped all Russian delegates could contribute to the discussions, but Komura wanted to limit the sessions to envoys, with secretaries and interpreters. The Japanese carried the day, agreeing only to Witte's request that certain delegates could come for special questions. As for language, it was English for the Japanese and French for the Russians. Witte generally spoke French except when he had trouble with a word and reverted to his native language: his remarks were then translated into Japanese. As the conference progressed he did tend to speak more in Russian, which Rosen translated into English. Despite Komura's fluency in English he usually spoke in Japanese with translation to French. Plenipotentiaries agreed that the treaty would be in English and French, with the French copy used in case of differences of interpretation. They decided to

22 Portsmouth *Herald,* Aug. 9, 1905.
23 Gaimusho, *Komura Gaikoshi,* II, 55-57.

draw up a daily protocol with annexes, to be approved at the succeeding meeting, showing business conducted and any agreement. They determined not to discuss the origins of the war—both sides were heartily in favor of this—and to discuss Japanese demands and Russian replies article by article, according to Roosevelt's suggestion that they discuss the most difficult terms last.[24] The president hoped this would create a climate for compromise.

One topic remained for this first session: secrecy of the meetings. The Japanese wanted secret proceedings. Witte did not. Even before leaving St. Petersburg the Russians had decided on open discussions. Some members of the court clique thought that if discussions were open the unacceptable Japanese demands would gain sympathy for the Russians. Witte was sure that if issues between the Japanese and the Russians were settled except, say, for the indemnity everyone thought Komura would demand, the Japanese cause—continuing the war for money—would be discredited before the world.[25] The Japanese again drove their point, and the delegates decided to hold sessions in private. The Russians had one recourse, for to Komura's irritation Witte frequently told newsmen of the negotiations.

THE CONFERENCE at Portsmouth in 1905 represented some of the most complex negotiations in modern peacemaking.[26] Only the meetings that ended the Korean War

[24] *Protokoly portsmutskoi mirnoi konferentsii i tekst dogovora mezhdu Rossieiu i Iaponieiu* [Protocols of the Portsmouth Peace Conference and Text of the Treaty Between Russia and Japan] (St. Petersburg, 1906), Aug. 9 and 10, 1905; hereafter cited as *Protokoly portsmutskoi mirnoi konferentsii;* see also Witte to Lamsdorff, Aug. 9, 1905 (#78), *Sbornik diplomaticheskikh dokumentov;* Gaimusho, *Komura Gaikoshi,* II, 58-60; and *Korostovetz Diary,* Aug. 9, 1905.

[25] *Korostovetz Diary,* Aug. 10, 1905.

[26] *Protokoly portsmutskoi mirnoi konferentsii,* Aug. 10, 1905; see also

of 1950-1953 could match the ensuing negotiation. Rarely have delegates come to a conference with a military situation so unsettled as was the case in August 1905. Little had happened since the battle of Tsushima. The Japanese had conquered Sakhalin but battlelines were approximately the same as after the victory at Mukden in March. The Russians seemed to be improving their position during this time without corresponding increases of strength by the Japanese. Japanese and Russians arrived at the conference hall on Thursday, August 10, and assumed battle stations: Komura on one side, with Takahira and Sato on his right and Ochiai and Adachi on his left; Witte on the other, with Nabokov and Planson on his right and Rosen and Korostovetz on his left. They would keep these places for the next four weeks. Each man would watch the others, looking for signs of strain such as nervousness or a declining resistance. Korostovetz noted that Witte fidgeted in his chair, crossed his legs, tore paper into little pieces, and twisted his feet; Komura gave away his more cool exterior by the manner in which he knocked ashes from cigarettes—hitting the table—and his manner of speech which became short and abrupt. The second plenipotentiaries said little in the discussions, occasionally talking with the chief delegates, though Baron Rosen sometimes offered suggestions that cooled tempers. As sessions progressed there were two slight changes in procedure. One, on Witte's suggestion, was the serving of tea during sittings, which added a relaxing touch. The other was that the delegates decided to eat breakfast at the navy yard, dinner being the only meal taken at the Wentworth.[27]

The session of August 10 opened like each succeeding

Witte to Lamsdorff, Aug. 10 (#81), and Aug. 12 (#83), 1905, *Sbornik diplomaticheskikh dokumentov;* Gaimusho, *Komura Gaikoshi,* II, 61-62.

[27] *Korostovetz Diary,* Aug. 10 and 16, 1905.

meeting, with the signing of protocols from the previous meeting. At this meeting, though, came the credentials, which the delegates exchanged. Looking at the Japanese documents Witte noted that the English version bore no signature vouching for the correctness of the translation, whereas Foreign Minister Lamsdorff had signed Russia's French translation. Komura replied that it was not the custom in Japan but if necessary he would sign the English version and this satisfied the Russian.[28] Next Witte remarked that Komura's credentials reserved for the Japanese emperor the right to review all decisions before ratification, in contrast to Russian credentials where there was no such condition. It was interesting that after all the fuss by the Japanese about the power of the Russian delegates, Witte came to Portsmouth with powers apparently stronger than those of the Japanese.[29]

The big moment then arrived. The room was silent. To Korostovetz the Japanese resembled sphinxes as Komura sat with a piece of paper in hand.[30] Komura broke the silence by announcing that the paper contained the Japanese demands for peace which were written in English in the form of clauses. He hoped the Russians would consider them carefully, giving a written reply to each. Witte accepted the paper and nonchalantly put it on the table, saying he would look at it and try to answer the clauses the following day.[31] He suggested a press re-

[28] *Protokoly portsmutskoi mirnoi konferentsii,* Aug. 10, 1905; Witte to Lamsdorff, Aug. 10, 1905 (#79) and (#80), *Sbornik diplomaticheskikh dokumentov;* Komura to Katsura, Aug. 11, 1905 (#13384), Telegram Series, Reels for 1905, Japanese Foreign Ministry Archives; Gaimusho, *Komura Gaikoshi,* II, 58-60; and *Korostovetz Diary,* Aug. 10, 1905.

[29] Portsmouth *Daily Chronicle,* Aug. 11, 1905—an article on the differences of the powers of the delegates appears in the paper; see also *Protokoly portsmutskoi mirnoi konferentsii,* Aug. 10, 1905; Kaneko to TR, Aug. 12, 1905, TR MSS: and Komura to Katsura, Aug. 11, 1905 (#13384), Telegram Series, Reels for 1905, Japanese Foreign Ministry Archives.

[30] *Korostovetz Diary,* Aug. 10, 1905.

[31] *Protokoly portsmutskoi mirnoi konferentsii,* Aug. 10, 1905; Witte

lease noting the exchange of credentials and presentation of peace terms. Komura approved and the Japanese withdrew, leaving the Russians to consider—in shirt sleeves because of the heat, no doubt one of the prime examples of shirt-sleeve diplomacy—the terms.

The demands called for Japanese control over Korea, evacuation of Russian troops from Manchuria, return to China of all occupied areas save the Liaotung peninsula, and acceptance of the open door. The Russians were to cede Sakhalin, transfer Port Arthur and Dalny as well as the railway between Harbin and Port Arthur, retain the Trans-Manchurian line subject to its use for non-military and nonaggressive purposes, pay expenses of the war, surrender all ships interned in neutral ports, limit naval strength in the Far East, grant fishing rights on the Russian Asiatic coast.[32] Noticeable was the fact that Komura's long trip and Roosevelt's urging had resulted in omission of the demand for destruction of the fortifications of Vladivostok and conversion of that city to a commercial port. The Japanese had begun to back down. Japan's uneasy military position had made Komura think of moderation.

The Russians worked until seven o'clock that evening. Witte thought it important that his delegation do this, to avoid the impression that he had to telegraph the demands to St. Petersburg and await a decision. With Nabokov reading the terms, Witte and staff drew up the Russian answers which Pokotilov and Shipov wrote down and Martens translated into French. They did not think the Japanese conditions would guarantee a lasting peace, in fact Martens thought that the Japanese terms would

---

to Lamsdorff, Aug. 10, 1905 (#81), *Sbornik diplomaticheskikh dokumentov; Korostovetz Diary,* Aug. 10, 1905; and Gaimusho, *Komura Gaikoshi,* II, 61-62.

32 *Protokoly portsmutskoi mirnoi konferentsii,* Aug. 10, 1905; and Gaimusho, *Komura Gaikoshi,* II, 61-62.

make a lasting peace an absolute impossibility. They talked about an agreement binding each power to defend the other's rights in the Far East. If the Japanese refused, Witte thought it probable that blame would fall on the Japanese. He determined to dispose of the less controversial demands: "we must on the contrary, act as broad-mindedly as possible in questions that are no material importance, and stand out for those conditions that are really important and show our compliance, so that in case of a rupture the blame should fall on the Japanese."[33]

The next day was uneventful. No sittings of the conference. The Russians did settle the final wording of their reply.[34] Unsolicited mail to the delegates continued, and one letter to Witte recalled the words supposedly spoken by the American envoy Charles C. Pinckney in Paris to Talleyrand during the XYZ Affair—"millions for defence [*sic*], but not one cent for tribute."[35]

When the Russians presented their reply on August 12, Komura and Witte started to match demands, replies, strategy, wits, bluffs, and sheer endurance. The Russian reply was in French, and the Japanese asked for time to translate. Komura turned to the press releases, noting that the accounts of the terms were partly fanciful. He thought that such revelation might cause great misunderstanding. He hoped there would be only official releases. Witte pointed out that some information had come from Tokyo, and said that the control of all leaks was impossible.[36] The Japanese did not press the point. In the

33 *Korostovetz Diary*, Aug. 10, 1905; and Witte to Lamsdorff, Aug. 15, 1905 (#99), *Sbornik diplomaticheskikh dokumentov.*

34 *Protokoly portsmutskoi mirnoi konferentsii*, Aug. 12, 1905; and Witte to Lamsdorff, Aug. 12, 1905 (#83), *Sbornik diplomaticheskikh dokumentov.*

35 *Korostovetz Diary*, Aug. 10, 1905.

36 Witte to Lamsdorff, Aug. 12, 1905 (#83), *Sbornik diplomaticheskikh dokumentov;* Komura to Katsura, Aug. 13, 1905 (#13433), Telegram Series, Reels for 1905, Japanese Foreign Ministry Archives; *Protokoly*

meantime, a message arrived from St. Petersburg indicating a harder line. The pressure on the tsar to continue the war was increasing. The tsar ordered Witte to refuse five Japanese terms: cession of Sakhalin, indemnity, giving up the South Manchurian railroad, transfer of interned ships, fishing rights. This caused Witte to ask Korostovetz to find out when the next steamer departed ("we shall probably sail in a few days time").[37]

That same afternoon arose the question of Korea. Witte used his rule of thumb—the Japanese could claim what their armies had conquered. The Russians agreed it was necessary to accept the Japanese demand. They recognized that the Japanese had paramount political, military, and economic interests in Korea, but demanded no impairment of the rights of the emperor of Korea. Without Witte's agreement Komura stated that the Japanese would maintain freedom of action. The delegates then compromised. The Japanese agreed that measures "in Korea in the future and which impair the sovereignty of that country will be taken in accord with the Korean government." The Japanese also accepted Witte's request of most-favored-nation treatment for Russian traders in Korea.[38] The session finished with everyone nervous and tired.

Next day, Sunday, no sittings, by mutual agreement. Witte and the Russians continued to court the American public. The Russians wanted to make good impressions. The Portsmouth *Herald* said that "if the Russians continue to mix and the Japanese to stay with the strict

portsmutskoi mirnoi konferentsii, Aug. 12, 1905; and *Korostovetz Diary,* Aug. 12, 1905.

37 Lamsdorff to Witte, Aug. 12, 1905 (#85), *Sbornik diplomaticheskikh dokumentov;* and *Korostovetz Diary,* Aug. 12, 1905.

38 *Protokoly portsmutskoi mirnoi konferentsii,* Aug. 12, 1905; Witte to Lamsdorff, Aug. 12 (#88), and Aug. 14, 1905 (#91) and (#92), *Sbornik diplomaticheskikh dokumentov;* Gaimusho, *Komura Gaikoshi,* II, 67-69; and *Korostovetz Diary,* Aug. 12, 1905.

business proposition, there will be an immense change in the public opinion of New Hampshire concerning the war. The envoys and their suites have been in the hotel thirty hours, and no one has seen a Japanese do a thing apart from the routine of business."[39] The paper noted the Russians already had a score of acquaintances, and one or another of them was always on hand when anything was going on about the hotel. The other Portsmouth paper, the *Daily Chronicle,* agreed: there was no doubt that the Russians had made a good impression.[40] Witte ordered the delegation to Christ Church in Portsmouth, telling Korostovetz it would make a good impression. On the same day Takahira and a colleague attended evening services. These visits led John Callan O'Laughlin, a correspondent for the Chicago *Tribune* who was close to Roosevelt and sent long letters to Oyster Bay, to write the president, "I wonder what the Lord thinks of such hypocrisy!"[41] Witte the following day received a group of Jewish bankers from New York including Oscar Straus, Isaac Seligman, and Jacob Schiff, and talked about the Jewish problem in Russia.[42]

Witte was convinced the Japanese would back down on small demands, but believed they would not desist from their principal demands.[43] The discussion turned to Manchuria and after pronouncements of both delegations as to the future of the Chinese, Komura and Witte considered the second and third demands concerning evacuation of troops and restoration to China of the occupied

[39] Portsmouth *Herald,* Aug. 11, 1905.

[40] Portsmouth *Daily Chronicle,* Aug. 17, 1905.

[41] *Korostovetz Diary,* Aug. 13, 1905; and O'Laughlin to TR, Aug. 13, 1905, TR MSS.

[42] *Korostovetz Diary,* Aug. 14, 1905; O'Laughlin to TR, Aug. 14, 1905, TR MSS; Straus to TR, Aug. 15, 1905, TR MSS; Isaac Seligman to TR, Aug. 17, 1905, and Jacob Schiff to TR, Aug. 18, 1905, TR MSS.

[43] Witte to Lamsdorff, Aug. 14, 1905 (#94) and (#95), *Sbornik diplomaticheskikh dokumentov.*

areas except the Liaotung lease. Komura in clear-cut sentences set forth the terms. Witte answered. To Korostovetz, Komura appeared less talented as a debater than Witte, but better prepared. More and more Komura's method impressed Korostovetz, in contrast to Witte's more emotional and inspirational appeals. Witte was too excited and talked too much.[44] The Russians maintained that they would evacuate their troops but not agree to impair the sovereign rights of China. The delegates agreed to evacuate and restore to the Chinese government all areas except Liaotung, and that such concessions as the Chinese Eastern railway did not violate Chinese integrity or the open door.[45]

The delegates had solved some minor questions. The major problems, which held the future of the conference, lay ahead.

44 *Korostovetz Diary,* Aug. 15, 1905.

45 *Protokoly portsmutskoi mirnoi konferentsii,* Aug. 14, 1905; Witte to Lamsdorff, Aug. 14 (#100) and 15 (#101), 1905, *Sbornik diplomaticheskikh dokumentov;* Gaimusho, *Komura Gaikoshi,* II, 69-70; and *Korostovetz Diary,* Aug. 14, 1905.

Chapter Eight

WAR OR PEACE

And now when ancient grandsires sit
Within the evening gray,—
And oysters frolic noisilee
All over Oyster Bay,
The graybeard tells his little niece
How Theodore did trek
To drag the gentle Bird of Peace
To Portsmouth—by the neck.[1]

ON AUGUST 15 the delegates began to discuss the crucial demands by talking about Sakhalin, a territory that Witte noted was a continuation of Russian possessions in Asia; it was about seven versts from the mainland. Witte maintained he was ready to make concessions only if they did not touch Russian honor. Komura made a long speech declaring that ancient Russian rights to Sakhalin did not antedate Japanese claims. Sakhalin he considered a question of national security to the Japanese, while to the Russians only a case of interest. For over 250 years the Japanese had authority over some part of the island, with the first appearance of officials there in 1624, in contrast to 1803 for the Russians. Russian occupation in 1850 was a lawless act, for Sakhalin was a continuation of the Japanese archipelago. Witte in turn recalled Japanese acknowledgment of Russian rights to the island in an 1875 treaty, in exchange for the Kurile Islands. He appreciated Japanese economic interest in the island, which he thought the chief reason for the demand for cession, but outlined Sakhalin's political and strategic importance:

"a watchman at our gates and Japan would like to be this watchman at her neighbour's door." He reminded the Japanese that German annexation of Alsace-Lorraine in 1871 was still a reason for hostility in Europe, whereas Bismarck's refusal to annex Austrian territory in 1866 had led to an alliance.[2]

Then came the question of indemnity. Like Sakhalin, this issue was a mixture of consideration and principle. In the private meeting of the Russian delegation on August 10 a long conversation had occurred, with Witte against payment. Only conquered lands, which Russia was not, he said, paid indemnity. Even if the Japanese gained much territory in Siberia the situation would not alter. He said that only poor countries paid an indemnity, and many bankers were ready to loan money to Russia—this, of course, was untrue. Hence "history shows us that even when the enemy was on Russian territory they did not find it possible to make such a demand." This logic resulted in the Russian reply to Komura that such a term would be negotiable only if the Japanese had taken Moscow.[3] Substituting the word *reimbursement* for *indemnity* also failed.[4]

Discussion moved to interned Russian vessels and limitation of Russia's Far Eastern naval power.[5] Komura was not satisfied with a Russian promise not to maintain large naval forces in eastern waters. He wanted a more

1 Hermann Hagedorn, *A Guide to Sagamore Hill* (New York, 1953), 33.

2 *Protokoly portsmutskoi mirnoi konferentsii,* Aug. 15, 1905; Witte to Lamsdorff, Aug. 15, 1905 (#102), *Sbornik diplomaticheskikh dokumentov; Korostovetz Diary,* Aug. 15, 1905; and Gaimusho [Foreign Ministry], *Komura Gaikoshi* [A History of Komura's Diplomacy], 2 vols. (Tokyo, 1953), II, 72-74.

3 *Korostovetz Diary,* Aug. 10 and 17, 1905.

4 *Ibid.,* Aug. 10, 1905.

5 *Protokoly portsmutskoi mirnoi konferentsii,* Aug. 17, 1905; Witte to Lamsdorff, Aug. 15 (#109), Aug. 17 (#118) and (#119), and Aug. 18, 1905 (#111), *Sbornik diplomaticheskikh dokumentov; Korostovetz Diary,* Aug. 17, 1905; and Gaimusho, *Komura Gaikoshi,* II, 84-87.

exact definition, and Witte refused. Witte reported to the Russian capital that he had reached no agreement with the Japanese on indemnity, interned vessels, naval power in the Far East, and Sakhalin, and if neither side would yield shortly the negotiation would break off. The tsar commented on this cable: "It was said—not an inch of land, not a rouble of indemnities. On this I will stand up to the end."[6]

Komura had come to Portsmouth under orders to try for everything. Witte's behavior throughout the conference was almost unbearable. At one point Komura exclaimed that Witte acted as if he represented the victors. The Russian only replied that there were no victors and therefore no defeated.[7] Such an attitude hardened the Japanese delegate's desire to force unpleasant terms. Witte suggested that the delegates discuss the remaining issue—fishing rights. Next day they did, deciding the Japanese could fish off the Russian coast but not in rivers or bays.[8]

PRESIDENT ROOSEVELT had not been comfortable sitting and reading and hearing the reports from Portsmouth, and as the negotiation became more rigid his concern grew. He was aware of the troubled negotiation, since Kaneko had visited him on August 7 and 14. The president also had been receiving letters from O'Laughlin, the newspaperman, who had contacts with the Russians. Meyer continued to draw an alarming picture in St. Petersburg, sure the war party was influencing the tsar.

[6] Witte to Lamsdorff, Aug. 16 (#112), Aug. 17 (#115), Aug. 18 (#123), and Aug. 19, 1905 (#124); see especially the tsar's comments on (#115) and (#123), *Sbornik diplomaticheskikh dokumentov.*

[7] Gaimusho, *Komura Gaikoshi,* II, 80.

[8] *Protokoly portsmutskoi mirnoi konferentsii,* Aug. 17 and 18, 1905; Witte to Lamsdorff, Aug. 17, 1905 (#120), *Sbornik diplomaticheskikh dokumentov.*

The ambassador reported the tsar's receiving petitions against a disgraceful peace. There was one from the clergy and the people of the five districts of Orenburg. Meyer was afraid the petitions would have considerable influence on the emperor but little on the Japanese.[9] The Russians, Meyer thought, would not pay an indemnity nor yield territory: "the plenipotentiaries are coming down to the hard nuts to crack & unless Japan gives way now in certain matters peace will not come about. Each appears to be firm & unyielding."[10]

The president thought he could get the Japanese to abandon two of the four troublesome articles—fleet limitations and transfer of interned vessels. He believed there would have to be an indemnity. It was nonsense for the Russians to expect the Japanese to give up Sakhalin. Roosevelt suspected that the Russians, especially Witte, were more interested in peace than they appeared. He wished to clear the Japanese of responsibility for any break, should one occur. He saw Kaneko again on August 18 at Oyster Bay and said he was prepared to make a personal appeal to the tsar and if necessary to the kaiser and the French president.[11] Roosevelt and Kaneko worked out the details of Roosevelt's appeal. If the appeal failed, Roosevelt was sure that public opinion would blame the Russians. Interestingly, the president and Kaneko had agreed on this strategy on August 7, two days after the opening reception at Oyster Bay.[12] Roosevelt now telegraphed Assistant Secretary Peirce ordering him to tell Witte that "I earnestly request that you send either Baron

9 Meyer to TR, Aug. 1, 1905, TR MSS.

10 Meyer Diary, Aug. 17, 1905, Meyer MSS LC.

11 Kaneko interview with TR, Aug. 18, 1905, "Kaneko Dan to Bei Daitōryō to no kaiken shimatsu," Kaneko Reel MT804, Japanese Foreign Ministry Archives; TR to Charles W. Eliot, Aug. 16, 1905, and TR to Kaneko, Aug. 22, 1905, TR MSS.

12 Kaneko interview with TR, Aug. 7, 1905, "Kaneko Dan to Bei Daitōryō to no kaiken shimatsu," Kaneko Reel MT804, Japanese Foreign Ministry Archives.

Rosen or some other gentleman who is in your confidence to see me immediately, so that I may through him send you a strictly confidential message."[13]

In Portsmouth meanwhile Komura decided on August 17 to give up lesser demands difficult to obtain, and cabled this plan to Tokyo.[14] The envoys talked in a private session the next day about a proposed compromise. Witte stated that he had received new instructions from St. Petersburg which left little choice but to let the negotiation fail. He wanted peace and if the Japanese had any reasonable proposal he would urge it on his government. He gave little hope to Komura when he declared that the attitude since his departure from St. Petersburg had turned in favor of continuing the war, as a result of Japanese insistence on territory and indemnity. He could go no further on indemnity than reimbursement for expenses incurred in caring for Russian prisoners. On Sakhalin he thought there might be some settlement: the northern part of the island had to remain Russian, since it was essential to the security of the Amur region; the southern part, which contained the center of the fishing industries, might go to Japan. Such a settlement would give the Japanese the Soya Straits, and the Russians would require a guarantee of freedom of navigation in that area.[15]

Komura reminded Witte of Japanese public opinion, for the people enjoyed the franchise and their views were more important than those of the Russian people. The Japanese people for over 50 years had wanted Sakhalin

[13] TR to Peirce, Aug. 18, 1905, containing TR to Witte, Aug. 18, 1905, SDA NA: see also Witte to Lamsdorff, Aug. 19, 1905 (#141), *Sbornik diplomaticheskikh dokumentov.*

[14] Komura to Katsura, Aug. 18, 1905, Gaimusho, *Komura Gaikoshi,* II, 87-90.

[15] *Protokoly portsmutskoi mirnoi konferentsii,* Aug. 18, 1905; Witte to Lamsdorff, Aug. 18, 1905 (#128) and (#129), *Sbornik diplomaticheskikh dokumentov; Korostovetz Diary,* Aug. 18, 1905; and Komura to Katsura, Aug. 18, 1905, Gaimusho, *Komura Gaikoshi,* II, 87-90.

and now thought the Russians also should cede part of Siberia. But Komura was ready to sacrifice excessive popular demands. Because Japanese troops had occupied Sakhalin, return of the northern half would require compensation. The plenipotentiary suggested 1.2 billion yen. Witte promised to telegraph the proposition to St. Petersburg. He did, and advised Lamsdorff that if the Russians wanted to blame the Japanese for failure of the conference they could not refuse to compromise on both these issues.[16] Lamsdorff replied that the offer did not hold much promise, since it violated the tsar's position on land and indemnity, but the foreign minister promised to submit it to the ministers of war, navy, and finance.[17]

Rooseveltian diplomacy behind the scenes increased to a feverish stage. Because of Roosevelt's note of August 18 to Witte, Peirce roused Rosen out of bed at 2:00 A.M. to read the president's request. The secretary suggested that if the Russian ambassador would take the 7:00 A.M. train for New York he could meet the *Sylph* at Bridgeport, Connecticut, completing the trip to Oyster Bay by afternoon, and see the president upon arrival. Peirce hoped Rosen would keep the trip a secret. Rosen set out early in the morning for the summer White House. Characteristically Roosevelt received Rosen while playing tennis in white flannels, speaking in intervals of the game. Apparently unaware of the Komura-Witte compromise of the day before, the president discussed the four troublesome demands. Three were no problem, since the Japanese would give up the demand for interned vessels and Russian fleet limitation and the Russians would have to accept Japanese possession of Sakhalin because troops had occupied it. The indemnity remained. This he would

16 Witte to Lamsdorff, Aug. 18, 1905 (#129), *Sbornik diplomaticheskikh dokumentov;* Gaimusho, *Komura Gaikoshi*, II, 87-90.

17 Lamsdorff to Witte, Aug. 20, 1905 (#132), *Sbornik diplomaticheskikh dokumentov.*

solve by conciliation, one advice-giver friendly to each country, such as President Loubet and King Edward VII. The suggestions would only be advice and not binding. Such a procedure would permit passions to cool, since it would take time. The president hoped Rosen would recommend this course to his government, not as a formal proposal from Roosevelt but as a suggestion in private conversation. The president compared Japanese occupation in Sakhalin to American possession of Panama: "We Americans are ensconsed at Panama and will not leave." Rosen was unimpressed. He answered that Japan was not the United States, and Russia especially was not comparable to Colombia. The Russian government would oppose the whole plan. The conversation broke up. A reporter recognized the ambassador at Bridgeport where he waited for the train for Portsmouth, and asked about the visit to the president, but Rosen remained silent.[18] The ambassador's analysis was correct, for when the plan was telegraphed to St. Petersburg, the tsar noted: "this measure will not lead to anything."[19]

Roosevelt told Jusserand his troubles. "Dealing with senators," he wrote, "is at times excellent training for the temper; but upon my word dealing with these peace envoys has been an even tougher job. To be polite and sympathetic and patient in explaining for the hundredth time something perfectly obvious, when what I really want to do is to give utterances to whoops of rage and jump up and knock their heads together—well, all I can hope is that the self-repression will be ultimately helpful for my character." When they drove him too nearly mad, he continued, he took refuge by reading about the treaty

[18] Witte to Lamsdorff, Aug. 19 (#141), and Aug. 20, 1905 (#142), *Sbornik diplomaticheskikh dokumentov;* Roman Rosen, *Forty Years of Diplomacy,* 2 vols. (New York, 1922), II, 269-71.

[19] Witte to Lamsdorff, Aug. 20, 1905 (#142), *Sbornik diplomaticheskikh dokumentov.*

between Ramses II and the Hittites, comparing it with Ramses' preposterous boasting over previous victories. Roosevelt felt that people of his time were not so far behind people of a few thousand years ago.[20]

To bring about direct negotiation the president now ordered Meyer to tell the emperor that Roosevelt was a well-wisher of Russia and would give similar advice were he a Russian patriot and statesman, that he had understood the Japanese had abandoned their terms for interned ships and limitation of Russian naval power in the Far East which even the president felt improper.[21] The Japanese had indicated willingness to restore northern Sakhalin in return for a substantial sum. He changed the Komura-Witte proposal so that the Russians would agree to the principle of paying for the northern part of the island. The exact amount could be negotiable. Peace on these terms would be just and honorable. To continue the war would be a dreadful calamity. Meanwhile Roosevelt reminded Witte how important the northern part of Sakhalin was for defending Vladivostok and eastern Siberia. Since there was no Russian navy, and Sakhalin was an island, negotiation seemed the only way to regain that part of it. Roosevelt hoped Witte would reinforce the appeal to the tsar. Witte did just that, writing St. Petersburg on August 21 that peace-loving public opinion would not side with the Russians on Sakhalin.[22] The Russians had no way to recover the island and could not refuse this demand in addition to paying no indemnity.

Roosevelt sent copies of his appeal to the French and German ambassadors in Washington, hoping the French

20 TR to Jusserand, Aug. 21, 1905, TR MSS.

21 TR to Meyer, Aug. 21, 1905, Meyer MSS.

22 TR to Witte, Aug. 21, 1905, TR MSS; and Witte to Lamsdorff, Aug. 21 (#143) and (#144), and Aug. 22, 1905 (#145) and (#146), *Sbornik diplomaticheskikh dokumentov.*

would urge their ally, Nicholas, to settle. He asked much the same from Kaiser Wilhelm through Speck von Sternburg. Concerned about Russian internal conditions and anxious to please Roosevelt, whose support he hoped for in the Moroccan crisis, the kaiser acted. A few days later the German emperor told his imperial cousin he had received a copy of Roosevelt's appeal and that as far as the kaiser could make out, the proposed compromise secured for the Russians all advantages of an honorable peace.[23]

Witte on August 22 received a cable from St. Petersburg stating that the Japanese were insisting on peace terms incompatible with Russian dignity. If the Japanese continued he was to cease negotiation. There was a great difference between forceful occupation of Sakhalin and cession of that island. From St. Petersburg came a second cable instructing him to tell the president of the Russian decision to break off negotiation. Another asked Witte for the closing date of the conference.[24] At this time, however, Witte asserted his independence. He refused to break off the negotiation until St. Petersburg officially answered the president's latest proposal.[25] In doing so Witte saved the conference.

Meyer saw the tsar late on the afternoon of August 23. According to the ambassador's diary the emperor's brick cottage was smaller than the Meyer summerhouse in Hamilton, Massachusetts. It was beautiful, since from

[23] TR to Jusserand, Aug. 21, 1905, and TR to Speck von Sternburg, Aug. 21, 1905, TR MSS; and Kaiser Wilhelm to Tsar Nicholas, Aug. 24, 1905, I. D. Levine, ed., *Letters from the Kaiser to the Czar* (New York, 1920); Hellmuth von Gerlach, ed., *Briefe und Telegramme Wilhelms II an Nikolaus II—1894-1914* (Berlin, 1920); and M. N. Pokrovsky, ed., *Perepiska Vilgelma vtorogo s Nikolaem vtorym* (Moscow, 1923).

[24] Witte to Lamsdorff, Aug. 20, 1905 (#142), and Lamsdorff to Witte, Aug. 22, 1905 (#147), (#148), and (#149), *Sbornik diplomaticheskikh dokumentov.*

[25] Witte to Lamsdorff, Aug. 22, 1905 (#152), *Sbornik diplomaticheskikh dokumentov.*

the windows one could throw a stone into the Gulf of Finland and could also see Kronstadt in the distance. Meyer noted how cordial the tsar was. After pleasantries, which included Meyer's displaying pictures of the Russian plenipotentiaries in Portsmouth, they turned to the matter of peace. Meyer was sure the emperor had prepared for certain questions but became perplexed at unexpected ones. The tsar appeared as a man of no force, no breadth of mind. Nicholas had the Russian capacity of passing off misfortunes and seeing things in the future. The tsar resorted to subterfuge, stating that his conscience told him what he had to do. Nicholas admitted he had a note from Kaiser Wilhelm urging peace. Remarking it was quite a coincidence that each time Meyer came to see him he received a telegram from the German emperor, Nicholas read part of his reply to Wilhelm. He had stated that much as he wanted peace it had to be honorable and could not include an indemnity or a territorial cession. Meyer believed that in a cabinet meeting the night before, the tsar had promised no payment. The ambassador wrote Roosevelt that if "I had managed to have seen him before he had any conference, I would have obtained from him, not an excessive amount, but a liberal amount in payment as purchase money." They then had talked about Sakhalin. On a map the ambassador pointed out how important the northern half of the island was and, since possession was nine points of the law, if the Russians did not accept division the whole island would be Japanese. When the straits froze, Nicholas replied, Russian troops would cross on the ice. Meyer said the Japanese fleet would surround the troops after the ice melted, and Nicholas admitted that a Russian navy capable of challenging the Japanese was twenty years away. The tsar declared that a division of Sakhalin would be an irritation. It might be better to continue the war. Showing the tsar the United States on the map, Meyer pointed to the boundary between Maine and Canada which was not the St. Lawrence River. Since the treaty of 1842, he said, there had been no trouble.[26] The tsar thereupon consented to division of Sakhalin.[27]

But the tsar refused an indemnity, for he considered payments for the northern half of the island to be a form of indemnity. The Russians were not vanquished, the Japanese not at the gates of St. Petersburg. He also asked Meyer why they had not attacked in Manchuria for four months. If it came to a question of money the Russian people would support his refusal, and he would go to the front and lead the army himself. The Russians had 500,000 men before the Japanese, and several thousand miles before St. Petersburg. Besides, the emperor wondered how any realistic price could be affixed to the northern part of Sakhalin. Meyer told Roosevelt that sentiment had increased for continuing the war. He recalled the Democratic party's victory after the McKinley tariff—Grover Cleveland's triumph in 1892. The Democrats had won on misrepresentation, he wrote, claiming that the peoples' pockets would suffer. The war party in Russia had similar success on the question of an indemnity. They had stirred public opinion to such an extent that the tsar had to refuse. It was surprising that he agreed to cede half of Sakhalin.[28]

[26] Meyer Diary, Aug. 23, 1905, Meyer MSS LC; Meyer to TR, Aug. 23 and 25, 1905, TR MSS; the letter talked about is from Kaiser Wilhelm to Tsar Nicholas, Aug. 24, 1905, Levine, *Letters from the Kaiser to the Czar;* von Gerlach, *Briefe und Telegramme Wilhelms II an Nikolaus II—1894-1914;* and Pokrovsky, *Perepiska Vilgelma vtorogo s Nikolaem vtorym.* Meyer was convinced that the Russians had broken the American code, which was true, but in this case the message was also sent by way of Witte.

[27] Meyer to TR, Aug. 23 and 25, 1905, TR MSS; and Russian Foreign Ministry Memorandum, Aug. 24, 1905 (#161), *Sbornik diplomaticheskikh dokumentov.*

[28] Meyer to TR, Aug. 25, 1905, TR MSS.

The president was not finished with the Russians. To Assistant Secretary Peirce he noted that Witte had not understood his message of August 21—the Russian delegate's response had proved that. Roosevelt maintained that reimbursement for north Sakhalin was not another form of indemnity, and advised the Russians to accept Komura's compromise.[29] To decline would be to invite a terrible disaster. He communicated further with Meyer and asked the ambassador to make clear that the price would be a subject of negotiation. Two days later he again cabled that continuing the war might "involve Russia in a greater calamity than has ever befallen it since it first rose to power in both Europe and Asia." If the Russians rejected the terms, the Japanese probably would take Vladivostok and Harbin. While the whole world desired peace, it was chiefly to Russian interests—perhaps vital interests—for peace to come.[30] The tsar noted on this appeal, "I remain with my views."[31]

Roosevelt simultaneously carried on discussions with the Japanese and their supporters, and to Kaneko he warned against continuing the war for a large indemnity. He had heard a good deal about such a possibility. A member of the Senate Foreign Relations Committee had written, he warned Kaneko, that one could not blame the Japanese for breaking off negotiations over Sakhalin. Their case on indemnity, the senator had said, was not good, since the only Russian territory they held was Sakhalin.[32] Japanese willingness to retrocede half of the island gave a chance to get some money from the Russians, though not a large sum. Roosevelt believed that public

[29] TR to Peirce, Aug. 23, 1905, SDA NA; Witte to TR, Aug. 22, 1905 (#146), *Sbornik diplomaticheskikh dokumentov* and TR MSS.

[30] TR to Meyer, Aug. 23 and 25, 1905, Meyer MSS. The cable begins, "My second cable was forwarded after the arrival of your first."

[31] Lamsdorff to Tsar Nicholas, Aug. 26, 1905, *Sbornik diplomaticheskikh dokumentov*.

[32] Lodge to TR, Aug. 21, 1905, TR MSS.

opinion would shift against the Japanese should the negotiation break up on an indemnity. The following day he again wrote Kaneko the same ideas.[33] The president enumerated Japanese successes: control of Korea and Manchuria, destruction of the fleet, and transfer of Port Arthur, Dalny, and the Manchurian railroad, and closed by stating: "ethically it seems to me that Japan owes a duty to the world at this crisis. The civilized world looks to her to make peace; the nations believe in her; let her show her leadership in matters ethical no less than in matters military. The appeal is made to her in the name of all that is lofty and noble; and to this appeal I hope she will not be deaf."

Roosevelt turned out a message to the British through Durand. To Durand he said that every friend of the Japanese should warn them against continuing the war for money, hoping that the British would urge the Japanese to make peace. To Henry White he noted his displeasure because the British were reluctant to advise the Japanese. In this respect, Roosevelt thought, they had not shown up well compared to the Germans and French.[34]

By this time nerves and tempers were getting jangled. On August 23 there was another meeting in Portsmouth, the first since August 18. Komura formally proposed the compromise, since accepted by Tokyo, but Witte's actions revealed the Russian position. Witte actually exceeded his instructions in the talk of the day. He asked whether Tokyo would give up all demands for money, if St. Petersburg would agree to cede the whole island of Sakhalin. Komura rejected such a proposal, probably unaware that the Russian had forced him into a position of willingness to continue the war for money alone. The delegates con-

[33] TR to Kaneko, Aug. 22 and 23, 1905, TR MSS; and Gaimusho, *Komura Gaikoshi,* II, 94-96.

[34] TR to Durand, Aug. 23, 1905, and TR to White, Aug. 23, 1905, TR MSS.

cluded the session by agreeing to reconvene on August 26, but the outlook was not hopeful.[35] Korostovetz was writing in his diary that all the Russians were sick of Portsmouth, especially the Wentworth Hotel, where the Russians thought there were too many journalists. Further, Witte had definite instructions and the war party to his dismay seemed to be convincing the tsar to continue the fight.

The president had also reached the end of his tether. Despite the well-nigh incredible number of letters from his office concerning the peace talks, there seemed to be little result. Roosevelt wrote Kermit, "I am having my hair turned gray by dealing with the Russian and Japanese peace negotiators. The Japanese ask too much, but the Russians are ten times worse than the Japs because they are so stupid and won't tell the truth."[36] The Japanese seemed most concerned. As a nation engaged in a struggle for national security and status among the powers, they had reached a place where victory was in sight, and felt abandoned by Roosevelt. Kaneko hastened to Oyster Bay on August 25, but got little satisfaction because Roosevelt pointed out that the United States had defeated Mexico and Spain and had not given them a hard time. Japan should do the same. In fact, for some unexplained reason Roosevelt did not tell Kaneko of Meyer's success, the tsar's willingness to cede the southern half of Sakhalin.[37] Perhaps he did not think it an important compromise. Perhaps Roosevelt had another

35 *Korostovetz Diary,* Aug. 23, 1905; and Gaimusho, *Komura Gaikoshi,* II, 98-101.

36 *Korostovetz Diary,* Aug. 18 and 24, 1905; and TR to Kermit Roosevelt, Aug. 25, 1905, TR MSS.

37 Kaneko interview with TR, Aug. 25, 1905, "Kaneko Dan to Bei Daitōryō to no kaiken shimatsu," Kaneko Reel MT804, Japanese Foreign Ministry Archives; and Gaimusho, *Komura Gaikoshi,* II, 97. Roosevelt probably just forgot. He never refers to it in writing but this is the interpretation the Japanese Foreign Ministry holds. Things were moving too fast.

event of the same day on his mind. One of the earliest submarines of the navy, the U.S.S. *Plunger,* had entered Oyster Bay. The president wanted to know how practical the sub was, sent for the young commander, and to the astonishment and horror of the Secret Service as well as his staff, had gone aboard the craft. For almost two hours the sub cruised under the waters of Long Island Sound. The president could not remember when he had had so much fun.

August 26 brought another meeting at Portsmouth, in which the prospects were not bright, for Witte told Korostovetz to get the hotel bill since he thought the delegation would leave shortly.[38] He commissioned one of the Russian secretaries to go to New York and take rooms. The sitting of that day began with another private meeting of the chief delegates in which Witte reiterated that the Russians would never pay an indemnity. By this time Witte had been informed by Lamsdorff of Meyer's success—the tsar's agreement to cede the southern part of the island of Sakhalin.[39] Witte hoped they would reach some compromise over Sakhalin, mentioned the Meyer solution, and said he was ready to do everything he could to achieve a compromise. He described the changing attitude in St. Petersburg in favor of war. The army was eager to renew the struggle. There was even some opposition in Russia to concessions made to the Japanese in respect to Manchuria. His government had not accepted Komura's proposal of three days earlier. Komura at this point asked for the formal Russian reply and for another postponement until the afternoon of August 28.[40] Komura sent a telegram to Tokyo, telling Katsura of the

[38] *Korostovetz Diary,* Aug. 26, 1905.

[39] Lamsdorff to Witte, Aug. 24, 1905 (#161), *Sbornik diplomaticheskikh dokumentov.*

[40] *Protokoly portsmutskoi mirnoi konferentsii,* Aug. 26, 1905; Gaimusho, *Komura Gaikoshi,* II, 99-105; and Witte to Lamsdorff, Aug. 23 (#160) and Aug. 26 (#177), 1905, *Sbornik diplomaticheskikh dokumentov.*

impasse.[41] He was concerned about what Witte had told him in private and related the conversation. He dealt with the possible consequences of the Russian decision to make no further compromise. Komura noted that neither his conciliatory attitude, which had led him to give up demands for interned ships and naval limitations, nor the appeals by the American president, had made any impression. Since further Japanese concessions would result in national humiliation, he proposed to bring negotiations to a halt on August 28 with a statement assigning full responsibility to the Russians.

Tokyo asked for another delay: this one for 24 hours, moving the next session to August 29. Takahira and one of the Japanese secretaries, Ochiai, visited Witte on the night of August 27 asking for the delay.[42] Because of the 14-hour time difference between Portsmouth and Tokyo, Komura still awaited instructions. Witte said the Russians had no objection to postponing the session but because they had no further concessions they did not want to waste time and hoped the next session would be the last. It became clear that the Japanese had a choice: accept Russian terms or end the negotiation. Komura cabled Tokyo reporting the conversation of Takahira and Witte and pointed out Witte's reasonable attitude in contrast to that of the Russian government.[43] It had come to the place where the original war aims were in doubt, since the gains in Manchuria had to have Chinese consent, and Russian pressure might cause difficulty there.

As for the Russians, a note from Lamsdorff ordered

[41] Komura to Katsura, Aug. 26, 1905, Gaimusho, *Komura Gaikoshi,* II, 105. Komura also sent another telegram on Aug. 27, 1905, to Katsura with much the same sentiments; see Gaimusho, *Komura Gaikoshi,* II, 107-108.

[42] Katsura to Komura, Aug. 27, 1905, and Komura to Katsura, Aug. 27, 1905, Gaimusho, *Komura Gaikoshi,* II, 106-108; and Witte to Lamsdorff, Aug. 27, 1905 (#178), *Sbornik diplomaticheskikh dokumentov.*

[43] Komura to Katsura, Aug. 27, 1905, Gaimusho, *Komura Gaikoshi,* II, 108-109.

Witte to break off negotiation, since all solutions had failed.[44]

The busiest person was still the president who made one more attempt for peace. The general manager of the Associated Press, Melville Stone, had suggested another possible solution: an appeal to Kaiser Wilhelm who would urge the tsar to compromise. The Japanese were to keep the southern part of Sakhalin. Stone talked to Kaneko but the baron said he would have to refer any proposal to Komura. Stone said he would go to the Lotus Club in New York City to prepare the message for Wilhelm and there would await word from Kaneko.[45] Later that evening—actually the next morning at 1:30 A.M.—Stone called Kaneko, asking him to come to the Lotus Club. Upon arrival and introduction to Baron Hilmar von dem Bussche-Haddenhausen, the German chargé who had come from Lenox, Massachusetts, on Stone's invitation, the three men prepared a message.[46] The communication asked Wilhelm to urge his cousin to compromise. Using the president's name the message began: "peace can be obtained on the following terms: Russia to pay no indemnity whatever and to receive back north half of Sakhalin for which it is to pay to Japan whatever amount a mixed commission may determine." The message said that Roosevelt had gained Japanese assent to the proposal and was sure the emperor could convince Nicholas to agree to it.

Kaneko telegraphed for Komura's approval, but the plenipotentiary only answered that in view of the Russian attitude nothing could come from such a proposal. Komura wrote Roosevelt saying that although the Japanese appreciated his earnest and sincere efforts, Komura

[44] Lamsdorff to Witte, Aug. 28 (#180) and Aug. 26, 1905 (#169), *Sbornik diplomaticheskikh dokumentov.*

[45] Loeb to Bussche-Haddenhausen, Aug. 27, 1905, TR MSS; and Kaneko to Melville Stone, Aug. 27, 1905, Gaimusho, *Komura Gaikoshi,* II, 121-22.

[46] TR to Kaiser Wilhelm, Aug. 27, 1905, TR MSS.

believed the latest appeal would fail. Trying to hurry the project, Stone asked a press representative at Portsmouth to inquire about Kaneko's authority. Takahira reportedly answered that the baron was not empowered to express any views independent of the plenipotentiaries. On hearing this Roosevelt telegraphed Komura that he had had interviews with Kaneko at the representative's request, on the assumption that Kaneko was acting with authority. Kaneko had forwarded copies of Japanese government telegrams for Roosevelt's information. The president had felt that all interchanges with Kaneko were with Komura's knowledge and permission: "I do not feel that Baron Kaneko should communicate with me any longer unless I am assured by you that it is your desire that he should do so and that he speaks with authorization from you." The chief Japanese delegate thereupon assured Roosevelt that the press reports were false. Komura wrote Takahira was fully aware that Kaneko was empowered to speak in Komura's name. Komura thanked the president for all he had done for peace.[47] Roosevelt then withdrew the proposed message to the kaiser.

Lines between Tokyo and Portsmouth were busy as the last session approached. Tokyo seemed more responsive to Roosevelt's urging for peace, for the Japanese government in contrast to the Russian was aware what continued fighting would mean. Komura received three cables on August 28 and 29 representing the last compromise by the Japanese.[48] From Tokyo Katsura instructed Komura to withdraw only the claim for an indemnity. If Witte refused, perhaps Roosevelt would ask the Japanese to withdraw their demand for Sakhalin, thus helping them save the government. But if the losing

[47] Komura to TR, in Kaneko to TR, Aug. 27, 1905, TR to Komura, Aug. 28, 1905, and Komura to TR, Aug. 29, 1905, TR MSS; and Gaimusho, *Komura Gaikoshi*, II, 122-24.

[48] Katsura to Komura, Aug. 28 and 29, 1905, Gaimusho, *Komura Gaikoshi*, II, 125-27.

of the peace was a possibility, Komura was to act alone, withdrawing both demands. Komura never had informed Tokyo of Witte's offer to cede the southern part of Sakhalin. But the situation was severe enough that the government wished to lose no opportunity to achieve peace and Komura was to be guided by this desire.[49]

About four hours later another cable followed, directing Komura to delay action on the earlier cable and await instructions. Kikujiro Ishii, head of the commercial bureau of the foreign office, told Kijuro Shidehara, head of the telegraphic section of the same office, of startling information. He had learned from the British minister in Tokyo, MacDonald, the substance of Meyer's visit of August 23 to the tsar.[50] The Russians would consent to the partitioning of Sakhalin. MacDonald could not give Ishii a copy of the London cable informing him of Meyer's success, but he read it to his Japanese friend twice. Ishii and Shidehara immediately brought this information to Katsura. Some of the members of the cabinet, for example Minister of the Navy Yamamoto, did not believe it. In the end Katsura accepted the information, though Ishii was said to have been reminded he would have to commit hara-kiri if it was wrong and the Japanese lost the peace. At 1:10 A.M. Tokyo time, August 29 (11:10 A.M. Portsmouth time, August 28), Katsura sent new instructions.[51]

The final day arrived. Negotiations were to break off if the crisis was not solved. Witte seemed prepared for a breakdown. A message from St. Petersburg called for a break. The tsar preferred to continue the war rather than "to await gracious concessions on the part of Japan." Nicholas seemed even to have regretted the concessions

49 Katsura to Komura, Aug. 28, 1905, Gaimusho, *Komura Gaikoshi,* II, 125-26.

50 Katsura to Komura, Aug. 29, 1905, Gaimusho, *Komura Gaikoshi,* II, 126-27.

51 *Ibid.*

Meyer had pulled from him. He told Witte to break off discussions no matter what Tokyo offered.[52] Witte was said to have prepared a signal to St. Petersburg: when he turned and asked for his Russian cigarettes, one of the secretaries would leave for the Wentworth to send the fateful cable. As for Roosevelt, he had spent himself in action, but now had to wait. The sitting of that day was preceded by another private meeting between the chief delegates in which the Russians learned of the Japanese decision.

The dramatic last formal meeting opened with Komura's announcing that the Japanese had as yet received no response to their compromise offer of August 23. Witte replied that his government, anyway, had turned down the offer. Komura said the Japanese would withdraw their demand for an indemnity if the Russians would cede Sakhalin. Witte refused.

Korostovetz recorded what happened next. Absolute silence reigned. Witte kept tearing up the paper lying beside him. Rosen was smoking. At last Komura, in a well-controlled voice, said that his government, having in mind peace and the bringing of the negotiation to a successful conclusion, accepted the Russian proposal to divide Sakhalin, without indemnity. Witte replied calmly that Russia accepted the Japanese proposal and that the fiftieth parallel would be the line of demarcation.[53] Again Witte had shown his independence and disobeyed the instructions from St. Petersburg.

52 Lamsdorff to Witte, Aug. 28, 1905 (#180), *Sbornik diplomaticheskikh dokumentov.*

53 *Korostovetz Diary,* Aug. 29, 1905; *Protokoly portsmutskoi mirnoi konferentsii,* Aug. 29, 1905; and Gaimusho, *Komuro Gaikoshi,* II, 128-29. While Witte certainly refused to obey instructions from Lamsdorff, and even telegraphed his intention to St. Petersburg, the tsar was nonetheless relieved at peace. The domestic situation was heating up again and no doubt Nicholas felt that with the war finished he could devote full attention to internal events.

Chapter Nine

ROOSEVELT AND THE TREATY

IN THIS BUILDING
at the invitation of
THEODORE ROOSEVELT,
PRESIDENT OF THE UNITED STATES
was held the
PEACE CONFERENCE
between the
ENVOYS OF RUSSIA AND JAPAN,
and
SEPTEMBER 5, 1905, at 3:47 P.M.,
was signed
THE TREATY OF PORTSMOUTH,
which ended the war between the two empires.[1]

ROOSEVELT DESCENDED the stairs at Oyster Bay holding a telegram in his hand and smiling from ear to ear. To Herbert Parsons, a longtime congressman from New York, he exclaimed that peace was a mighty good thing for Russia and Japan, adding it was a "mighty good thing for me too."[2] In Japan the treaty met violent opposition. On September 5 in Tokyo's Hibiya Park there was a mass protest meeting. That night and the next day riots flared.[3] Reception in Russia, less violent, was just as unpopular. Witte became known as Count Half-Sakhalin. In both countries, however, the governments realized Roosevelt's accomplishment. So did others, for the American president won the 1906 Nobel Peace Prize.

It was clearly a Roosevelt-managed peace. The conference had assembled on his initiative. He had convinced the Japanese and the Russians of the need for it.

Although the war would have ended sometime, it seems that peace would have been precious long in coming if Roosevelt had not been at work. His preaching made the powers think of moderate terms. His influence was especially apparent on the Japanese, since he had convinced Komura to modify the terms even before the conference. Roosevelt kept the conference going by constant contact with the plenipotentiaries and their governments. After the Russian government decided to renew the military operations it seems that Roosevelt's urging through Meyer brought about the necessary compromises, though by that time the Japanese were ready to make peace even without the compromises.

For the Japanese the treaty was a victory, for it gained all the war aims. The Russians had been forced back from Manchuria and Korea, and though the concessions at Portsmouth attached Chinese acceptance as a requirement this was not a major problem. After Portsmouth the Japanese held the necessary talks in Peking which assured their position in China.[4] Komura had conducted himself well, and only the unrealistic expectations of the uninformed Japanese populace soured the reception of the treaty in Japan. In the broader picture this war made the Japanese a major power. The spectacular victories over the Russians had propelled the nation to the fore of all decisions involving the Far East. And the peace gave the Japanese time to consolidate their gains.

The Russians escaped from the peace with more than

1 Commemorative plaque on the "Peace Building" at the Portsmouth Navy Yard.

2 Undated memo of Anson P. Stokes, Stokes MSS.

3 Griscom to Root, Sept. 15, 1905, TR MSS. Griscom assured Washington that the riots were against the methods police used in dealing with the demonstrators, but the demonstration was called to protest the treaty.

4 For the Peking negotiations, see John White, *The Diplomacy of the Russo-Japanese War* (Princeton, 1964).

the tsar could have hoped. They had to give up their ambitions in the Far East. They lost Korea and their Far Eastern fleet. They had been defeated in major battles, and only the better sense of the Japanese had saved them from disaster. This is not to say that Japan could have conquered Russia. But a continued war, its expense, and internal unrest would have presented strains on an overtaxed monarchy. Witte proved himself a remarkable negotiator. He had fought with tenacity, partly by bluff and bluster, partly by the course of events, to convince the Tokyo government, though possibly not Komura, that the Russians would make no further concessions. He had won another battle—that with the tsar and especially with the faction of the Russian government which recklessly urged a continuation of the war. If he had to resort to disobedience to win, in the long run the peace gave Russia some chance for experiment in democracy, unfortunately cut short in 1917.

The treaty's importance to the United States lessened in the years that followed, as the new Rooseveltian power balance in the Far East collapsed. But all this was the result of alignments looking toward the World War. In the Russo-Japanese treaties of 1907 and 1910 the two powers agreed to divide Manchuria by control of the two Manchurian railways. The open door in Manchuria now closed. The war of 1904-1905 had given Japan control of Korea. Russia was in Inner Mongolia. It was sheer coincidence that the immigration policy in the United States at this time became an issue of domestic politics, and it, of course, had a bad effect on American-Japanese relations.

The pro-Japanese feeling of the State Department disappeared when Theodore Roosevelt left the White House. Washington took to protecting the Chinese, as in the absurd proposal of Secretary of State Philander C. Knox to neutralize the railroads in Manchuria. American foreign policy became known as dollar diplomacy, and the United States seemed to engage the Japanese in competition for the supposedly lucrative Chinese markets. The Japanese showed little desire to share commerce in their spheres of influence. And there was a change in China, a new nationalism, opposed to foreigners. Roosevelt had discounted this possibility; he viewed the Chinese as a backward people incapable of controlling their country. For this and other reasons Roosevelt's policy failed.[5]

Roosevelt's mediation, one must conclude in perhaps wistful retrospect, marked the last time a great international dispute proved susceptible to personal arrangement. His momentary success closed the diplomacy of the nineteenth century. After 1905 foreign affairs became impersonal, gaining a kind of inevitability that proved almost impervious to mediators. President Woodrow Wilson in 1916 sought to mediate the World War, to no avail. Twenty-three years later President Franklin D. Roosevelt sent frantic letters to the European nations in an attempt to avoid the Second World War. But Theodore Roosevelt succeeded, and thus his work of 1904 and 1905 takes on special interest for the historian. He was an unusual person. John Morley was correct in calling Roosevelt and Niagara Falls the two outstanding natural phenomena in America.

[5] Howard K. Beale, *Theodore Roosevelt and the Rise of America to World Power* (Baltimore, 1956), 332-34.

APPENDIX

Ratification of the Treaty of Peace Signed at Portsmouth August 23, 1905, between Russia and Japan[1]

By the helping grace of God, we, Nicholas II, Emperor and Autocrat of all the Russias etc., hereby declare that, in consequence of a mutual agreement between us and His Majesty, the Emperor of Japan, our plenipotentiaries concluded and signed at Portsmouth, August 23, 1905, a treaty of peace which, word for word reads as follows:[2]

His Majesty, the Emperor of all the Russias, on the one hand, and His Majesty, the Emperor of Japan, on the other hand, being animated by the desire to restore the benefits of peace for their countries and their peoples, have decided to conclude a treaty of peace and have appointed for this purpose their plenipotentiaries, to wit:

His Majesty the Emperor of Russia—

His Excellency, Mr. Sergius Witte, his secretary of state and president of the committee of ministers of the Empire of Russia, and

His Excellency, Baron Roman Rosen, master of the Imperial Court of Russia and his ambassador extraordinary and plenipotentiary to the United States of America;

And His Majesty, the Emperor of Japan—

His Excellency, Baron Komura Iutaro, Iusammi, knight of the Imperial Order of the Rising Sun, his minister of foreign affairs, and

His Excellency, Mr. Takahira Kogoro, Iusammi, knight of the Imperial Order of the Sacred Treasure, his envoy extraordinary and minister plenipotentiary to the United States of America;

Who, after having exchanged their full powers, found in good and due form, concluded the following articles:

ARTICLE ONE

There shall be in the future peace and friendship between Their Majesties the Emperor of all the Russias and the Emperor of Japan, as well as between their respective nations and subjects.

ARTICLE TWO

The Imperial Government of Russia, recognizing that Japan has predominant political, military, and economic interests in Korea, agrees not to interfere or place obstacles in the way of any measure of direction, protection, and supervision which the Imperial Government of Japan may deem necessary to adopt in Korea.

It is agreed that Russian subjects in Korea shall be treated in exactly the same manner as citizens of other foreign countries; that is, that they shall be placed on the same footing as the citizens of the most-favored nation.

It is likewise agreed that, in order to avoid any cause of misunderstanding, the two high contracting parties shall refrain from adopting, on the Russo-Korean frontier, any military measures which might menace the security of the Russian or Korean territory.

ARTICLE THREE

Russia and Japan mutually engage:

1. To completely and simultaneously evacuate Man-

[1] Enclosure in Meyer to Root, Dec. 13, 1905, SDA NA; for the French version, see *Protokoly portsmutskoi mirnoi konferentsii,* 97-107.

[2] This date is Russian style: in western style it is Sept. 5, 1905.

churia, with the exception of the territory over which the lease of the peninsula of Liaotung extends, in accordance with the provisions of additional Article I annexed to this treaty, and

2. To entirely and completely restore to the exclusive administration of China all parts of Manchuria now occupied by Russian and Japanese troops, or which are under their control, with the exception of the above-mentioned territory.

The Imperial Government of Russia declares that it has no territorial advantages or preferential or exclusive concessions in Manchuria of such a nature as to impair the sovereignty of China or which are incompatible with the principle of equal opportunity.

ARTICLE FOUR

Russia and Japan mutually pledge themselves not to place any obstacle in the way of general measures which apply equally to all nations and which China might adopt for the development of commerce and industry in Manchuria.

ARTICLE FIVE

The Imperial Government of Russia cedes to the Imperial Government of Japan, with the consent of the Government of China, the lease of Port Arthur, of Talien, and of the adjacent territories and territorial waters, as well as the rights, privileges, and concessions connected with this lease or forming part thereof, and it likewise cedes to the Imperial Government of Japan all the public works and property within the territory over which the above-mentioned lease extends.

The high contracting parties mutually engage to obtain

from the Government of China the consent mentioned in the foregoing clause.

The Imperial Government of Japan gives on its part the assurance that the property rights of Russian subjects within the above-mentioned territory shall be absolutely respected.

ARTICLE SIX

The Imperial Government of Russia obligates itself to yield to the Imperial Government of Japan, without compensation and with the consent of the Chinese Government, the Chan-chun (Kwan-Chien-Tsi) and Port Arthur Railroad and all its branches, with all the rights, privileges, and property thereunto belonging within this region, as well as all the coal mines in said region belonging to this railroad or being operated for its benefit.

The two high contracting parties mutually pledge themselves to obtain from the Chinese Government the consent mentioned in the foregoing clause.

ARTICLE SEVEN

Russia and Japan agree to operate their respective railroads in Manchuria for commercial and industrial purposes exclusively, but by no means for strategic purposes.

It is agreed that this restriction does not apply to the railroads within the territory covered by the lease of the Liao-tung peninsula.

ARTICLE EIGHT

The Imperial Governments of Russia and Japan, with a view to favoring and facilitating relations and traffic, shall conclude, as soon as possible, a separate convention to govern their operations of repair on the railroads in Manchuria.

ARTICLE NINE

The Imperial Government of Russia cedes to the Imperial Government of Japan, in perpetuity and full sovereignty, the southern part of the island of Saghalin, and all the islands adjacent thereto, as well as all the public works and property there situated. The fiftieth parallel of north latitude is adopted as the limit of the ceded territory. The exact boundary line of this territory shall be determined in accordance with the provisions of additional Article II annexed to this treaty.

Japan and Russia mutually agree not to construct within their respective possessions on the island of Saghalin, and the islands adjacent thereto, any fortification or similar military work. They likewise mutually agree not to adopt any military measures which might hinder the free navigation of the Straits of La Perouse and Tartary.

ARTICLE TEN

The right is reserved to Russian subjects inhabiting the territory ceded to Japan to sell their real property and return to their country; however, if they prefer to remain in the ceded territory, they shall be guarded and protected in the full enjoyment of their property rights and the exercise of their industries provided they submit to the laws and jurisdiction of Japan. Japan shall have perfect liberty to withdraw the right of residence in this territory from all inhabitants laboring under political or administrative incapacity, or to deport them from this territory. It pledges itself, however, to fully respect the property rights of these inhabitants.

ARTICLE ELEVEN

Russia obligates itself to reach an understanding with Japan in order to grant Japanese subjects fishing rights along the coast of the Russian possessions in the Seas of Japan, Okhotsk, and Bering.

It is agreed that the above-mentioned obligations shall not impair the rights already belonging to Russian or foreign subjects in these regions.

ARTICLE TWELVE

The treaty of commerce and navigation between Russia and Japan having been annulled by the war, the Imperial Governments of Russia and Japan agree to adopt as a basis for their commercial relations, until the conclusion of a new treaty of commerce and navigation on the basis of the treaty in force before the present war, the system of reciprocity on the principle of the most favored nation, including import and export tariffs, custom-house formalities, transit and tonnage dues, and the admission and treatment of the agents, subjects, and vessels of one country in the territory of the other.

ARTICLE THIRTEEN

As soon as possible after the present treaty takes effect, all prisoners of war shall be mutually returned. The Imperial Governments of Russia and Japan shall each appoint a special commissioner to take charge of the prisoners. All prisoners in the custody of one of the governments shall be delivered to the commissioner of the other government or to his duly authorized representative, who shall receive them in such number and in such suitable ports of the surrendering nation as the latter shall notify in advance to the commissioner of the receiving nation.

The governments of Russia and Japan shall present to each other, as soon as possible after the delivery of the prisoners has been completed, a verified account of the direct expenditures made by them respectively for the care and maintenance of the prisoners from the date of capture or surrender until the date of their death or return. Russia agrees to refund to Japan, as soon as possible after the exchange of these accounts, as above stipulated, the difference between the actual amount thus spent by Japan and the actual amount likewise expended by Russia.

ARTICLE FOURTEEN

The present treaty shall be ratified by Their Majesties the Emperor of all the Russias and the Emperor of Japan. This ratification shall, within the shortest possible time and at all events not later than fifty days from the date of the signature of the treaty, be notified to the Imperial Governments of Russia and Japan, respectively, through the ambassador of the United States of America at St. Petersburg and the minister of France at Tokyo, and from and after the date of the last of these notifications this treaty shall enter into full force in all its parts.

The formal exchange of the ratifications shall take place at Washington as soon as possible.

ARTICLE FIFTEEN

The present treaty shall be signed in duplicate, in the French and English languages. The two texts are absolutely alike; however, in case of difference of interpretation the French text shall prevail.

In witness thereof the respective plenipotentiaries have signed the present treaty of peace and affixed thereto their seals.

Done at Portsmouth, New Hampshire, the twenty-third day of August (fifth of September) of the year one thousand nine hundred and five, corresponding to the fifth day of the ninth month of the thirty-eighth year of Meiji.

IUTARO KOMURA. [L.S.]
K. TAKAHIRA. [L.S.]
SERGIUS WITTE. [L.S.]
ROSEN. [L.S.]

In conformity with the provisions of Article II [*sic*—III] and IX of the treaty of peace between Russia and Japan under this date, the undersigned plenipotentiaries have concluded the following additional articles:

1. TO ARTICLE THREE:

The Imperial Governments of Russia and Japan mutually agree to begin the withdrawal of their military forces from the territory of Manchuria simultaneously and immediately after the entrance into force of the treaty of peace; and within a period of eighteen months from this date the armies of the two powers shall be entirely withdrawn from Manchuria, with the exception of the leased territory of the peninsula of Liao-tung.

The forces of the two powers occupying advanced positions shall be withdrawn first.

The high contracting parties reserve the right to maintain guards for the protection of their respective railroad lines in Manchuria.

The number of these guards shall not exceed 15 men

per kilometer, and within the limit of this maximum number the commanders of the Russian and Japanese armies shall, by mutual agreement, fix the number of guards who are to be employed, this number being as low as possible and in accordance with actual requirements. The commanders of the Russian and Japanese forces in Manchuria shall reach an understanding regarding all the details connected with the evacuation, in conformity with the principles herein above set forth, and shall, by mutual agreement, adopt the measures necessary to carry out the evacuation as soon as possible and at all events within a period not exceeding eighteen months.

II. To article nine:

As soon as possible after the present treaty takes effect, a boundary commission composed of an equal number of members appointed respectively by the two high contracting parties shall mark on the spot and in a permanent manner the exact line between the Russian and Japanese possessions on the island of Saghalin. The commission shall be obliged, as far as topographical conditions permit, to follow the 50th parallel of north latitude for the line of demarcation, and in case any deviations from this line are found necessary at certain points compensation shall be made therefor by making corresponding deviations at other points. It shall also be the duty of said commission to prepare a list and description of the adjacent islands which are comprised within the cession, and finally the commission shall prepare and sign maps showing the boundaries of the ceded territory. The labors of the commission shall be submitted to the approval of the high contracting parties.

The additional articles mentioned hereinabove shall be considered as being ratified by the ratification of the treaty of peace, to which they are annexed.

Portsmouth, August 23 (September 5), 1905, corresponding to the 5th day, 9th month, and the 28th [*sic*—38th] year of Meiji.

IUTARO KOMURA.
K. TAKAHIRA.
SERGIUS WITTE.
ROSEN.

Bibliographical Essay

Because of the importance of the Russo-Japanese War, its peace, and the participation in these events by Theodore Roosevelt, the sources for this present study proved almost massive. This essay cites the most important, either bibliographical, background, secondary works, or primary material.

BIBLIOGRAPHICAL AIDS

The best guide to American diplomacy is Samuel Flagg Bemis and Grace Gardner Griffin, *Guide to the Diplomatic History of the United States, 1775-1921* (Washington, 1935). Though old, it is still the most extensive listing. Also helpful are Oscar Handlin and others, *Harvard Guide to American History* (Cambridge, Mass., 1954); and Elmer Plischke, *American Foreign Relations: A Bibliography of Official Sources* (College Park, Md., 1955).

For the Russian side there are many important bibliographies, compiled both by Russians and Americans. The general Soviet guides are headed by two bibliographies issued by Knizhnaya Palata: *Mezhdunarodnoe polozhenie: ukazatel literatury* [The International Situation: Index of the Literature] (Moscow, 1939); and *Ukazatel' literatury po mezhdunarodnomy polozheniiu* [Index of the Literature on the International Situation] (Moscow, 1940). More special Soviet bibliographies include the Central Archive, *Russkie finansy i evropeiskaia birzha v 1904-1906* [Russian Finances and European Markets, 1904-1906] (Moscow, 1926); G. K. Derman, *Pervaia russkaia revoliutsiia: ukazatel literatury* [The First Russian Revolution 1905: Index of the Literature] (Moscow, 1930); Ivan A. Senchenko, *Ocherki istorii Sakhalina;*

vtoraia polovina XIX v., nachalo XX v. [Historical Studies on Sakhalin during the Second Half of the 19th Century and the Beginning of the 20th Century] (Moscow, 1957); and especially Vladimir V. Luchinin, *Russko-iaponskaia voina, 1904-1905 gg; ukazatel knizhnoi literatury na russkom i inostrannykh iazykakh* [The Russo-Japanese War of 1904-1905: Index to Literature in Russian and Foreign Languages] (Moscow, 1940). The latter is indispensable. One should note the Library of Congress, *Monthly Index of Russian Accessions* (Washington, 1948-), which lists new Soviet titles. Of American guides to Russian materials, most important are Charles Morley, ed., *Guide to Research in Russian History* (Syracuse, 1951); Paul Horecky, *Russia and the Soviet Union* (Chicago, 1965); Robert F. Byrnes, ed., *A Modest Preliminary Guide to Materials on Russian History in the Nineteenth and Twentieth Century* (Bloomington, Ind., 1961); and Fritz T. Epstein, "Russia and the Soviet Union," *Guide to Historical Literature* (New York, 1961). Another worthy publication is Tung-li Yuan, "Russian Works on Japan—A Selected Bibliography," *Monumenta Serica,* XIX (1960), 403-36. Less helpful are Robert Kerner, *Slavic Europe* (Cambridge, Mass., 1918); and Robert Kerner, *Northeastern Asia: A Selected Bibliography,* 2 vols. (Berkeley, 1939). Anyone doing research on Russia should consult the New York Public Library, *Catalog of the Slavic Collection* (Boston, 1959), a handy guide indexed by subject, author, and title.

Bibliographies on Japan for this study are by western compilers. The two standard bibliographical works on Japanese history of this era are Friedrich von Wenckstern, *A Bibliography of the Japanese Empire,* 2 vols. (Tokyo, 1907); and Oskar Nachod, *Bibliography of the Japanese Empire, 1906-1926,* 2 vols, (London, 1928). Both include extensive listings in Japanese. See also John W. Hall, *Japanese History: A Guide to Japanese Reference and*

Research Materials (Ann Arbor, 1954); Hugh Borton and others, *A Selected List of Books and Articles on Japan in English, French and German* (Cambridge, Mass., 1954); Bernard Silberman, *Japan and Korea: A Critical Bibliography* (Tucson, 1962); and Hugh Borton and John W. Hall, "Japan," *Guide to Historical Literature* (New York, 1961). A researcher should consult the New York Public Library, *Catalog of the Oriental Collection* (Boston, 1960).

GENERAL WORKS

General accounts of the diplomacy of this period, all valuable for the broader picture, include Rene Albrecht-Carrié, *A Diplomatic History of Europe Since the Congress of Vienna* (New York, 1958); Hugh Seton-Watson, *The Decline of Imperial Russia* (New York, 1956); Sidney B. Fay, *The Origins of the World War,* 2 vols. (New York, 1928); and Harley MacNair and Donald Lach, *Modern Far Eastern International Relations* (New York, 1955). The last has the best bibliography. For Soviet interpretations there is *Diplomaticheskii slovar* [Diplomatic Dictionary], 2 vols. (Moscow, 1948). Vladimir P. Potemkin, *Istoriia diplomatii* [A History of Diplomacy], 3 vols. (Moscow, 1945) deals only briefly with the Russo-Japanese War, condemning the Russians for imperialism in the Far East, at the same time discussing the "dastardly" Japanese attack on Port Arthur. Finally one must mention Mark Sullivan, *Our Times,* 6 vols. (New York, 1927-1935), colorful description of the years 1900-1925, invaluable for this period of American history.

SPECIAL WORKS

Monographs Monographs on America's relationship to the Russo-Japanese War are plentiful but of varied value. The four best are Raymond A. Esthus, *Theodore Roosevelt and Japan* (Seattle, 1966); William H. Harbaugh, *Power and Responsibility: The Life and Times of Theodore Roosevelt* (New York, 1961); Howard K. Beale, *Theodore Roosevelt and the Rise of America to World Power* (Baltimore, 1956); and Tyler Dennett, *Roosevelt and the Russo-Japanese War* (Garden City, N. Y., 1925). All deal with the peace in some detail, with Esthus's treatment the most recent and complete. One notch below but still valuable are A. L. P. Dennis, *Adventures in American Diplomacy, 1896-1906* (New York, 1928); A. W. Griswold, *The Far Eastern Policy of the United States* (New York, 1938); and an excellent article by Nelson M. Blake, "Ambassadors at the Court of Theodore Roosevelt," *Mississippi Valley Historical Review,* XLII (1955), 179-206.

Perhaps the best studies of Russia are Robert K. Godwin, "Russia and the Portsmouth Peace Conference," *American Slavic and East European Review,* IX (1950), 279-91; and Ernest R. May, "The Far Eastern Policy of the United States in the Period of the Russo-Japanese War: A Russian View," *American Historical Review,* LXII (1957), 345-51. American-Russian relations appear in Edward Zabriskie, *American-Russian Rivalry in the Far East: A Study in Diplomacy and Power Politics, 1895-1914* (Philadelphia, 1946); Pauline Tompkins, *American-Russian Relations in the Far East* (New York, 1949)—a highly critical look at American policy which the author describes as youthful in this era; Andrei Lobanov-Rostovsky, *Russia and Asia* (Ann Arbor, 1951); David Dallin, *The Rise of Russia in Asia* (New Haven, 1949); Thomas A. Bailey, *America Faces Russia* (Ithaca, 1950); and more briefly in William A. Williams, *American-Russian Relations 1781-1947* (New York, 1952); David S. Crist, "Russia's Far Eastern Policy in the Making," *Journal of Modern History,* XIV (1942), 317-41; and Georges Michon, *The*

Franco-Russian Alliance, 1891-1917 (New York, 1929). The most recent study, John A. White, *The Diplomacy of the Russo-Japanese War* (Princeton, 1964), is quite disappointing. The book is based primarily on printed sources. Especially noticeable is the dependence on published materials for American participation in the peace settlement. As a result, despite much material, the study contributes little new information.

One Soviet historian, Boris A. Romanov, has written much on the Russo-Japanese War and the Portsmouth Peace Conference. In *Russia in Manchuria, 1892-1906,* trans. Susan W. Jones (Ann Arbor, 1952), he condemns the foreign policy of Tsarist Russia in the "epoch of imperialism," but does not consider the peace. Another of his books, *Ocherki diplomaticheskoi istorii russko-iaponskoi voiny, 1895-1907* [A Survey of the Diplomatic History of the Russo-Japanese War, 1895-1907] (Moscow, 1947), has a long section on Portsmouth. Soviets have done other work in this area, such as L. N. Kutakov, *Portsmutskii mirnyi dogovor: iz istorii otnoshenii Iaponii s Rossiei i SSSR, 1905-1945* [The Portsmouth Treaty: From the History of Japanese Relations with Russia and the USSR, 1905-1945] (Moscow, 1962); Aleksandr S. Dobrov, *Dal'nevostochnaia politika SShA v period russko-iaponskoi voiny* [The Far Eastern Policy of the United States during the Russo-Japanese War] (Moscow, 1952); A. Galperin, *Anglo-iaponskii soiuz, 1902-1921* [Anglo-Japanese Alliance from 1902 to 1921] (Moscow, 1947); Pavel P. Sevostianov, *Ekspansionistskaia politika SShA na Dal'nem Vostoke; v Kitae i Koree v 1905-1911 gg.* [The Expansionist Policy of the United States in the Far East, China and Korea in 1905-1911] (Moscow, 1958); and Emelian Iaroslavsky, *Russko-iaponskaia voina i otnoshenie k nei bolshevikov* [The Russo-Japanese War and the Attitude of the Bolsheviks to It] (Moscow, 1939).

As for secondary material on Japan, see Hyman Kublin,

"The Japanese Socialists and the Russo-Japanese War," *Journal of Modern History,* XXII (1950), 322-39; Ian H. Nish, *The Anglo-Japanese Alliance: The Diplomacy of Two Island Empires, 1894-1907* (London, 1966); Tatsuji Takeuchi, *War and Diplomacy in the Japanese Empire* (New York, 1935); and Gataro Ogawa, *Expenditures of the Russo-Japanese War* (New York, 1923). All describe Japan at the time of the treaty. Kublin's article shows the struggle between the Socialists, who advocated universal peace, and the Japanese government. Harold Phelps Stokes, brother of the secretary of Yale University, published *Yale, the Portsmouth Treaty, and Japan* (Lenox, Mass., 1948), a summary of the Stokes MSS in the Sterling Memorial Library at Yale. Other studies touching on Japanese-American relations are Payson J. Treat, *Japan and the United States, 1853-1921* (Stanford, 1928); and his more special *Diplomatic Relations Between the United States and Japan, 1895-1905* (Stanford, 1938); Foster Rhea Dulles, *Forty Years of American-Japanese Relations* (New York, 1937); and Rebecca Brooks Gruver, *Japanese-American Relations 1900-1934* (Berkeley, 1956). All have helpful bibliographies. Less important is Roy H. Akagi, *Japan's Foreign Relations, 1542-1936: A Short History* (Tokyo, 1936).

Winston B. Thorson attempts to refute the idea of Witte's shift of opinion in "American Public Opinion and the Portsmouth Peace Conference," *American Historical Review,* LIII (1948), 439-64; an enlargement of "Pacific Northwest Opinion on the Russo-Japanese War of 1904-1905," *Pacific Northwest Quarterly,* XXV (1944), 309-27. His thesis is that American public opinion was strongly pro-Japanese throughout the war and the peace. Evidence indicates that Witte's determined effort to win public opinion did meet with some success, perhaps not causing a drastic shift. Interesting questions of international law are in Amos S. Hershey, *The International Law and Diplomacy of the Russo-Japanese War* (New York, 1906); and Frederick Birkenhead and N. W. Sibley, *International Law as Interpreted During the Russo-Japanese War* (London, 1907). Hershey's book has a chapter on the peace.

Two of the most interesting unpublished doctoral dissertations on topics closely related to the Peace of Portsmouth are Edgar Stewart, "American Foreign Policy Incident to the Russo-Japanese War 1904-1905" (University of California, 1939); and Henry Whitney, "British Foreign Policy in the Russo-Japanese War" (University of Pennsylvania, 1948). Others include Wei-ping Tsai, "The Russo-Japanese Conflict in the Far East" (University of Illinois, 1938); Victor Petrov, "Manchuria as an Objective of Russian Foreign Policy" (American University, 1954); Harold Ford, "Russian Far Eastern Diplomacy, Count Witte, and the Penetration of China, 1895-1904" (University of Chicago, 1950); and David Crist, "Russia's Manchurian Policy, 1895-1905" (University of Michigan, 1940).

Autobiographies and Biographies Roosevelt's *An Autobiography* (New York, 1920) contains views of men in the negotiation, especially Meyer and Kaneko. In addition, biographies such as Henry F. Pringle, *Theodore Roosevelt: A Biography* (New York, 1931); George E. Mowry, *The Era of Theodore Roosevelt, 1900–1912* (New York, 1958); Tyler Dennett, *John Hay* (New York, 1933); and Allan Nevins, *Henry White* (New York, 1930), all relate Theodore Roosevelt's mediation. Then there is M. A. De Wolfe Howe, *George von Lengerke Meyer* (New York, 1920), a poor substitute for the rich Meyer manuscripts and diaries. Also Lloyd C. Griscom, *Diplomatically Speaking* (Boston, 1940); Edward Martin, *The*

Life of Joseph H. Choate (New York, 1927); and Royal Cortissoz, *The Life of Whitelaw Reid,* 2 vols. (London, 1921).

For the Russian side, see Sergei Witte, *Vospominaniia* [Memoirs], 2 vols. (Berlin, 1922; reissued in 3 vols., Moscow, 1960). An abridged English edition is *Memoirs of Count Witte* (New York, 1921), ed. Abraham Yarmolinsky. The sections dealing with the United States also appeared in *World's Work,* XLI (1921), entitled "Count Witte's Memoirs—My Visit to America and the Portsmouth Peace Conference." One must be careful in using Witte's recollections. Baron Rosen contributed *Forty Years of Diplomacy,* 2 vols. (New York, 1922). See also V. N. Kokovtsov, *Out of My Past* (Stanford, 1935), useful for the tsar's attitude on peace. Other Russian memoirs are Charles Seegar, ed., *The Memoirs of Alexander Iswolsky: Formerly Russian Minister of Foreign Affairs and Ambassador to France* (London, 1920); A. Savinsky, *Recollections of a Russian Diplomat* (London, 1928); and the British journalist E. J. Dillon, *The Eclipse of Russia* (New York, 1918). Probably the most important Russian memoir is Ivan Korostovetz, "The Peace Negotiations at Portsmouth—A Diary by I. Ia. Korostovetz," *Byloe* [The Past], VII, VIII, and IX (1917); later translated as *Pre-war Diplomacy; the Russo-Japanese Problem; Treaty Signed at Portsmouth, U.S.A.* (London, 1920); and still later published as *Stranitsa iz istorii russkoi diplomatii. Russko-iaponskie peregovory v Portsmute v 1905* [A Page from the History of Russian Diplomacy. The Russo-Japanese Negotiations at Portsmouth in 1905] (Peking, 1923). This is indispensable because Korostovetz was Witte's secretary and was present at almost every meeting of the delegates. Korostovetz excels in description, giving the little details so often missing in diplomatic history.

For some reason the Japanese lagged in memoir material. Baron Kentaro Kaneko published *Nichiro seneki hiroku* [Secret Records of the Russo-Japanese War] (Tokyo, 1929), but it is a summary of material in the Japanese Foreign Ministry Archives. Two helpful volumes are *The Secret Memoirs of Count Tadasu Hayashi,* trans. Alfred M. Pooley (New York, 1915); and *The Diplomatic Commentaries of Viscount Kikujiro Ishii,* trans. William R. Langdon (Baltimore, 1936).

Useful is Jules Jusserand, *What Me Befell* (Boston, 1933), letters and interesting remarks about Roosevelt and Witte. Two other French works are Maurice Bompard, *Mon Ambassade en Russie 1903-1908* (Paris, 1937); and Georges Maurice Paléologue, *Three Critical Years 1904-05-06* (New York, 1957). Both describe France's efforts to save Russia. The German material comes as a result of the close relation between the two emperors. Many of Ambassador Speck von Sternburg's letters, as well as those between the kaiser and his ministers, appear in Geoffrey Dunlop, *Memoirs of Prince von Bülow 1903-1909,* 4 vols. (Boston, 1931); and Oakley Williams, trans., *Prince Bülow and the Kaiser* (London, 1932). On the British side, Percy Sykes, *The Right Honourable Sir Mortimer Durand* (London, 1926) is of little value; but Roosevelt's use of his friend Spring Rice makes Stephen Gwynn, *The Letters and Friendships of Sir Cecil Spring Rice,* 2 vols. (New York, 1929) the most important British study. Also good is Thomas Newton, *Lord Lansdowne: A Biography* (London, 1929).

American journalists took special interest in the peace. Thomas F. Millard in *The New Far East* (New York, 1906) presents a sympathetic case for China, condemning Russia, Japan, and the United States as aggressors. A close friend of Roosevelt's, Melville E. Stone, wrote *In Associated Press M.E.S.* (New York, 1918), which lists conversations with delegates.

Newspapers and Periodicals Any student of American diplomacy in the twentieth century quickly acquires a debt to the New York *Times,* probably the most complete American paper, full of all sorts of information. Portsmouth newspapers at this time, the *Herald,* and *Daily Chronicle,* are helpful, strong in local color, from such things as menus to minute-by-minute diplomatic accounts. Dispatches of the diplomats were full of press clippings. Meyer's reports contained articles from Russian papers. Reports of Griscom had clippings from the Japanese press. Telegrams and dispatches to Tokyo gave excerpts from papers in America, Britain, France, and Germany. All Japanese diplomats reported public opinion to Tokyo. Especially diligent were Takahira in Washington and Inouye in Berlin.

Periodicals of the day covered the peace conference in detail. E. J. Dillon published many articles: "The Official Narrative of the Peace Conference," *Harper's Weekly,* XLIX (1905), 1334-37; "The Peace Conference at Portsmouth, N. H.," *Harper's Weekly,* XLIX (1905), 1222-24; "Sergius Witte," *The American Monthly Review of Reviews,* XXXII (1905), 292-95; "Sergius Witte and Jutaro Komura," *Harper's Weekly,* XLIX (1905), 1262-64, 1279; "The Story of the Peace Negotiations," *The Contemporary Review,* LXXXVIII (1905), 457-78; and "What the Peace of Portsmouth Means to Russia," *Harper's Weekly,* XLIX (1905), 1337, 1351. Other examples are Thomas F. Millard, "The Fruits of Japan's Victory," *Scribner's Magazine,* XXXVIII (1905), 240-51; and Melville E. Stone, "The Portsmouth Conference," *The Saturday Evening Post,* CLXXXVII (1915), 3-4, 48.

Printed Sources For correspondence concerning the outbreak of the war one should consult Vladimir Burtzev,

Tsar i vneshniaia politika; vinovniki russko-iaponskoi voiny po tainym dokumentam: Tainaia zapiska Gr. Lamsdorfa i malinovaia kniga [The Tsar and Foreign Policy; The Perpetrators of the Russo-Japanese War in Secret Documents: Secret Memorandum of Count Lamsdorff and the Crimson Book] (Berlin, 1910). Turning to the peace, there is the Ministry of Foreign Affairs, *Protokoly portsmutskoi mirnoi konferentsii i tekst dogovora mezhdu Rossieiu i Iaponieiu* [Protocols of the Portsmouth Peace Conference and Text of the Treaty Between Russia and Japan] (St. Petersburg, 1906), formal minutes signed at the beginning of each session for the preceding one. Ministry of Foreign Affairs, *Sbornik diplomaticheskikh dokumentov kasaiushchikhsia peregovorov mezhdu Rossieiu i Iaponieiu o zakliuchenii mirnago dogovora 24 maia-3 oktiabria* [Collection of Diplomatic Documents Concerning Negotiations Between Russia and Japan About the Conclusion of the Peace Treaty May 24-October 3] (St. Petersburg, 1906), is the most valuable Russian publication on the peace. Apparently available in the United States only at the New York Public Library and Indiana University, it contains the complete correspondence between Witte and Lamsdorff. Interesting are marginal notations of Tsar Nicholas II on many of Witte's telegrams and the memoranda prepared for the emperor by the Foreign Ministry. Finally there are letters published by the Soviets under the title "Portsmouth Correspondence of S. Iu. Witte and Others," in *Krasnyi arkhiv* [Red Archives], 106 vols. (Moscow, 1922-1941), VI and VII (1924). These letters mostly are not to Lamsdorff but to Kokovtsov. Parenthetically one must note Leonid S. Rubinshek, *Digest of the Krasnyi arkhiv, Volumes 1-30* (Cleveland, 1947); and Leona W. Eisele, *Digest of the Krasnyi arkhiv, Volumes 31-106* (Ann Arbor, 1955).

Japanese published sources are less extensive than the

Russian. The Foreign Ministry published *Nihon Gaiko Nempyo narabi Shuyo monjo* [Japanese Diplomatic Chronology and Principal Documents], 2 vols. (Tokyo, 1955), but it is too general. More helpful for outbreak of the war is Japanese Imperial Diet, *Correspondence Regarding the Negotiations Between Japan and Russia (1903-1904)* (Washington, 1904), material available in the Foreign Ministry Telegram Series. As for the Peace Conference, the Japanese government (like the Russian) published *Protocoles de la conférence de la paix entre le Japon et la Russie* (Tokyo, 1906). Due to the shortcomings of the Telegram Series, to be explained shortly, one must turn to Gaimusho (Foreign Ministry), *Komura Gaikoshi* [A History of Komura's Diplomacy], 2 vols. (Tokyo, 1953); this Foreign Ministry work fills the gap—the missing telegrams are in these volumes.

Because of involvement of major neutral European powers—Britain, France, and Germany—the documents of these countries are worth attention. See the well-known *British Documents on the Origins of the War, 1898-1914,* 11 vols. (London, 1926-1938); *Documents diplomatiques français 1871-1914,* 31 vols. (Paris, 1929-1959); and *Die Grosse Politik der Europäischen Kabinette, 1871-1914,* 40 vols. (Berlin, 1922-1927).

There are countless editions of Roosevelt letters. The best by far is Elting E. Morison, *The Letters of Theodore Roosevelt,* 8 vols. (Cambridge, Mass., 1951-1954). See also Joseph B. Bishop, *Theodore Roosevelt and His Time: Shown in His Own Letters,* 2 vols. (New York, 1920); and Will Irwin, *Letters to Kermit from Theodore Roosevelt 1902-1908* (New York, 1946).

Fascinating is the series of letters exchanged by Tsar Nicholas and Kaiser Wilhelm. The useful collections are Isaac Don Levine, ed., *Letters from the Kaiser to the Czar* (New York, 1920); Hellmuth von Gerlach, ed.,

Briefe und Telegramme Wilhelms II an Nikolaus II—1894-1914 (Berlin, 1920); and M. N. Pokrovsky, ed., *Perepiska Vilgelma vtorogo s Nikolaem vtorym* [Letters of Wilhelm II with Nicholas II] (Moscow, 1923). Levine's is the most reliable, since the kaiser wrote in English, but the other two are more extensive, containing some of the tsar's replies. Other letter collections worth examining include Herman Bernstein, *The Willy-Nicky Correspondence* (New York, 1918); Sidney B. Fay, "The Kaiser's Secret Negotiations with the Czar 1904-1905," *American Historical Review,* XXIV (1918), 48-72; "Russian-German Relations, 1905," *Krasnyi arkhiv,* V (1924); and Frederic Whyte, ed., *Letters of Prince von Bülow 1903-1909* (London, 1930).

MANUSCRIPT SOURCES

Archives A starting place for research on American diplomatic history is the State Department records in the National Archives, containing much material such as "Dispatches from U.S. Diplomatic Personnel Abroad," "Notes to Foreign Legations in the United States from the Secretary of State," "Diplomatic Instructions of the Department of State," and "Notes from Foreign Legations in the United States." Department records are available on microfilm, indexed in *List of National Archives Microfilm Publications: 1966* (Washington, 1966). Some appear in *Foreign Relations of the United States* for 1903-1904-1905 (Washington, 1904-1906). Most useful are the records of the Department of the Navy in the National Archives: "Records of the Secretary of the Navy," "Official Papers of the Portsmouth Navy Yard," and the logs of the ships that took part in the preconference festivities.

Valuable are the Archives of the Japanese Foreign Office microfilmed by the American government after capture in 1945. See Cecil H. Uyehara, *Checklist of Archives in the Japanese Ministry of Foreign Affairs, Tokyo, Japan, 1868-1945* (Washington, 1954). The archives contain much on diplomacy of the Russo-Japanese War and the Treaty of Portsmouth: there are over 43,000 pages of telegrams to and from Foreign Minister Komura for 1904 and 1905. A good portion involve Takahira in Washington. Unfortunately, as negotiation reached critical stages one encounters blank sheets listing names of correspondents—one wonders if the Japanese destroyed these items before the 1945 surrender. Other portions of the archives make up for this shortcoming. Valuable is "Nichi-Ro Sen'eki kankei kakkoku yoron keihatsu no tame Suematsu, Kaneko ryō-Danshaku Ōbei e haken ikken" [Documents Relating to the Despatch of Barons Suematsu and Kaneko to Europe and the U.S. for the Purpose of Enlightening Public Opinion in Various Countries Regarding the Russo-Japanese War]. One interesting section of this series is "Kaneko Dan to Bei Daitōryō to no kaiken shimatsu" [Interviews between Baron Kaneko and the President of the United States], probably the most important Japanese source on the Treaty of Portsmouth, Kaneko's account of frequent interviews with Roosevelt, showing what the president hoped to accomplish and exactly how pro-Japanese he was. This section also contains "Kaneko Dan no Tai-Bei nikki" [Baron Kaneko's Diary of his Sojourn in the U.S.] and "Kaneko Dan no hōkoku" [Baron Kaneko's Report], intimate pictures of the baron's dealings with the American president as well as his relations with the Yale faculty.

Personal Papers Any study of the Treaty of Portsmouth has to begin with the Theodore Roosevelt MSS in the

Manuscript Division of the Library of Congress, which are extensive and important: he acted as his own secretary of state, and communications ordinarily kept in the State Department archives appear here. The papers contain correspondence with Russians and Japanese as well as the French, Germans, and British. Next in importance are the George von L. Meyer MSS in the Massachusetts Historical Society and the Meyer Diaries for 1904-1905-1906 in the Library of Congress, a remarkable picture of internal Russian conditions and the large part in the diplomacy taken by Meyer. See also the William Howard Taft MSS and John Hay MSS, especially Hay's Diaries for 1904-1905, in the Library of Congress, and the Henry Cabot Lodge MSS in the Massachusetts Historical Society. Other MSS collections used in this study are those of Elihu Root, Lloyd Griscom, Oscar Straus, Joseph Choate, Henry White, and Whitelaw Reid in the Library of Congress, and Charlemagne Tower in the Columbia University Library. The Horace Porter MSS in the Library of Congress make little mention of Portsmouth. The Anson Phelps Stokes MSS in the Sterling Memorial Library at Yale give that university's side of an episode in diplomatic history. See also the Swarthmore College Peace Collection, a valuable source for many topics in twentieth-century American diplomatic history.

Index